HYPNO-TISING

HYPNO-TIZING

THE SECRETS & SCIENCE
OF ADS THAT SELL MORE...

DR. MARK YOUNG

HOUNDSTOOTH
PRESS

HYPNO-TISING

The Secrets and Science of Ads That Sell More...

ISBN   978-1-5445-2611-9 *Hardcover*

978-1-5445-2609-6 *Paperback*

978-1-5445-2610-2 *Ebook*

This book is dedicated to every client who ever
trusted us with the future of their business.

You created the opportunities for real-world learning.

CONTENTS

PREFACE

Nothing about me as a child was normal. I always had an insatiable desire to learn about business and science. Like many 11-year-olds, I spent my after-school time at home alone while my parents were busy trying to make a living. I started to learn about advertising and became enthralled with it. Like most kids, I did not know what I did not know, so I opened up the Yellow Pages (for the younger generations, it was a big, yellow book where you looked up names and phone numbers to businesses) and started to call advertising agencies trying to get a job in the business.

As you can well imagine, I never got past the receptionist at any agency, except one. It was a small, specialty advertising company that sold what many in the business refer to as "trash and trinkets." The owner of this firm was intrigued by an 11-year-old wanting to be in the business and asked if he could meet with my parents.

My parents were used to odd things happening with and around me, so they agreed to let Mr. Spiceland call on them. He offered me a job, commission only, selling ad specialties. There it was; I had arrived. I was now an ad man.

My uniqueness as a young kid working in an adult world made me an anomaly, and people found it hard to say no to a child. I quickly became a top producer, many weeks outearning my own parents. I was in love with the world of business and advertising, and just as important, I was fascinated by what motivated people to do the things they do.

Since those days, my adult career path has covered many areas: musician, police officer, martial arts instructor, radio host, commercial actor, contractor, engineer, real estate developer, entrepreneur, advertising strategist, creative director, and a Doctor of Psychology. The common thread throughout all these vocations has been the ability to understand what people think and feel and to persuade them to my way of thinking.

For the past 25-plus years, I have been creating advertising that moves people to take action. I ultimately opened my own advertising agency in the mid-90s, which is now called Jekyll and Hyde Labs. In my years of owning an agency, I have studied the works of other marketers, applied some common sense, made some mistakes, and helped turn clients' products into winners, selling billions of dollars in products and, in some cases, even helping them reach the #1 position in their category. But even so, I have never thought that my learning was complete. In fact, the more I learned, the more successful I became, so I continue to learn today.

I look forward to sharing some of that knowledge with you and am inspired by the thought of what it may do for your future.

Are you ready to learn how your marketing efforts can become much more effective?

THE GOAL OF ADVERTISING

The goal of every advertiser should be to maximize the results or investment in advertising while providing legitimate information to consumers.

Great communications should be crafted in a fashion that will help consumers overcome their own built-in biases and fears and lean into the mental shortcuts or heuristics of the consumer and motivate them to explore life-improving products and services.

Dr. Richard Bandler points out in several of his writings that the biggest human fear is the fear of change—what some refer to as the unknown. This fear of change is what keeps people stuck in negative situations. It is the old adage of

"Better the devil you know than the devil you don't." This is the reason why a woman stays in an abusive relationship fearing life alone or without him, why the alcoholic fears change to a life without drinking, or why the worker stays stuck in a dead-end job for fear of the unknown, or the change to a new career (*Richard Bandler Live Webinar*, 2019).

This same fear of change drives consumers to continue to purchase the same goods and services even if they are inferior to new and more innovative products. This fear of change or the unknown, in many cases, prevents people from changing to the products or services that will benefit their life.

While these fears exist, they are not typically conscious or considered decisions. In fact, people frequently do not make buying decisions for logical reasons. In many cases, individuals do not even realize or understand why they purchase the things that they do.

This book addresses the role of the unconscious mind in terms of processing power compared to the conscious mind and demonstrates that by using neuro-linguistic programming (NLP), hypnotic patterns, and behavioral science, marketers can leverage those nonlogical buying triggers or reasons.

II

WHY HYPNO-TISING?

Where did we get the term Hypno-tising? As both a doctor specializing in clinical hypnotherapy and the CEO of a successful advertising agency, I can give you the short answer: it is a combination of Hypnosis and Advertising. But let us look deeper at the origin.

First, "Hypno" is from the word "hypnosis." Most people's first exposure to hypnosis is watching a live stage hypnosis show or seeing it on television. If you are like most people, you have always wondered, "Is hypnosis actually real?" and "Are those 'volunteers' on stage real or just plants?" Let me assure you that hypnosis is real, and the volunteers are not plants. What you see in a stage hypnosis show is 100 percent legitimate. The stage hypnotist is quickly using suggestibility testing to discover which of the volunteers are most susceptible to his suggestions. Then he quietly has the remaining volunteers go back to their seats. From there, the stage hypnotist can induce the volunteers to do nearly anything, provided it does not violate their personal values or beliefs.

While similar to stage hypnosis, hypnotherapy is the discipline of using words, images, and guided messaging to cause an immediate change in a person's behavior. Unlike traditional therapy, hypnotherapy is immediate. The changes take place at once during a single session.

Next comes "-tising," from the word "advertising." Let us examine good advertising. Advertising by its very nature is using works, images, and messaging to cause an immediate change in "buying" behavior. In other words, good advertising is hypnotic.

It is the goal of every advertiser and marketer to improve the results of advertising and commercial communications. My introduction to NLP and hypnosis was motivated by the desire to communicate better, to reach people at a deeper and more emotional level, and to create copy and messaging that motivates people to take immediate action.

I have spent decades of my life dedicated to communicating advertising messages to the public. During this time, I have had the opportunity to experiment with many different types of messaging and creativity. I have had a front row seat to witness what worked and what did not.

WHY DO WE NEED HYPNOTIC LANGUAGE IN ADVERTISING?

In our agency, we've often seen clients who have a product or service that will benefit people, so they believe that just informing the general public will lead to sales. Unfortunately, that's simply not the case.

A major issue that marketers face today is one of advertising clutter. A study by Media Dynamics shows that the average person is exposed to 5,000 to 20,000 advertising messages per day. Not all of these come in the form of a TV or radio ad. Many are web based, or outdoor signage. To compound the flood of media, we have packaging that is advertising to us. A simple walk in the spaghetti sauce aisle will give you up to 50-plus different ad impressions just for that one simple item.

But the challenge is even bigger than just this. Media Dynamics' research shows us that if we assume the lower number of 5,000 ad impressions per day, the average person will receive 362 of them. Out of this, only 153 will actually be noted.

Of the 153, only 86 will have any level of awareness, meaning the consumer recognizes or acknowledges the message. Now here is the really bad news: out of the 86, only 12 of them will make an impression, which does not mean the consumer actually responded to the offer.

Every advertiser's goal should be to land in the 12 messages that a consumer has a reaction to and to motivate that consumer to take action. To improve the odds of doing so, we can use the techniques of hypnotherapists. They reach past the conscious mind to the unconscious mind and help make immediate changes in behavior and belief systems. Imagine your advertising having the same type of authority as that (and NLP) to change the way a person thinks and feels after seeing your message. How powerful would that be?

So, when we think of Hypno-tising, we are using words and images to create an immediate change in a person's behavior.

THE CONCERNS ABOUT NEUROSCIENCE IN ADVERTISING

Some people challenge the ethics of using subliminal techniques to influence people to make a choice of one product over another. There have been some activists that have called for an abandonment of the use of neuroscience in advertising. The claim is that it is wrong for marketers to use such techniques to persuade the public to buy products or services (Stanton et al., 2014). Their fear, however unfounded, is that these techniques could be used to sell products that are of no value to the consumer. However, we see evidence that regardless of the underlying techniques employed in communications, it is nearly impossible to sell a product to someone who has no need for it. To put it simply, you're never going to be able to sell arthritis medicine or treatments to someone who does not suffer from arthritis—no matter what advertising technique you utilize.

The activists' argument is that advertising communications should be limited to descriptive narratives, where the only information being shared consists of simple facts or details about the given subject.

The execution of such a practice would be nearly impossible. First, who would be the governing body responsible for monitoring or passing judgment on this? Second, imagine the sheer volume of advertising messages being created on a daily basis. This would number into the millions. Developing a workforce with the high level of skill and education necessary to review every communication would literally be impossible.

Finally, what would be the criteria for approval? One person's opinion of a metaphor could well be another person's artistic portrayal. And if hypnotic language is as covert as these detractors claim it is, how would they even detect it?

The Supreme Court case Jacobellis v. Ohio is a good demonstration of how impossible this task would be. In 1963, Nico Jacobellis was charged with two counts of possession and exhibiting obscene material in his Ohio movie theater.

Jacobellis was found guilty by the Cuyahoga County Court

and the conviction was upheld by the Ohio Court of Appeals and the Ohio Supreme Court. The case eventually made its way to the US Supreme Court based on a violation of constitutional rights.

The Supreme Court ruled that the film was not obscene. The point to follow here is that there were four different opinions written, not including the majority opinion, and that no single opinion had more than two justices in agreement.

One of the most famous of these opinions was written by Justice Potter, when he said that he could not describe what pornography is, but he would know it when he saw it.

If nine Supreme Court justices cannot agree on the definition of pornography, it is doubtful that you would ever create a standard to identify the difference between information and persuasion.

The truth is all the advertising in the world will not keep bad products or services alive for long. You just cannot sell products to people who do not identify them as a need! So, it really is difficult to sell air conditioning at the North Pole or get someone to buy dog food when they do not own a dog. In contrast to this, we see that people have many complex, underlying issues and fears and that these fears often prevent a person from exploring new products or possibilities that will improve the quality of their lives.

To summarize: The goal is not to sell people things they do not want or need. The true goal of great advertising is to inform potential customers who have a need for the product or service that a new solution to their need exists, and to help them overcome their own resistance to change.

By using NLP and improving the ability to persuade people to embrace or accept change, we can improve their lives while providing an improved business atmosphere for deserving companies that have made innovative products.

HOW THE BRAIN SEES ADVERTISING

SEVEN BITS: THE UNCONSCIOUS MIND CALLS THE SHOTS

Before we get into how the brain experiences advertising messages, we must first recognize that as marketers our advertising messages are much more important to us than they are to the average consumer. People typically see advertising as a passive activity. They are not hyper-focused on every word and do not see them the way we, the creators of the ads, see them.

GRAPES, DIMES, AND BEACH BALLS

To understand how the brain works, we need to focus on the difference between the conscious and unconscious mind.

Imagine the conscious mind is represented by a grape. The grape is sitting on a dime. Now imagine the grape and the dime are on top of a beach ball (Miller, 1956).

This is a visual representation of our minds. The grape reflects how our conscious mind can handle seven bits of information, plus or minus two. This is why phone numbers are seven digits. Phone numbers are based on the number of digits the average person can remember.

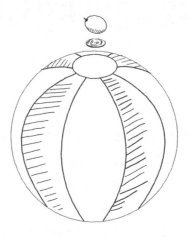

The dime represents the critical facility, or the brain's ability to process and examine information. Finally, the beach ball represents the unconscious mind, which can handle thousands of bits of information simultaneously.

As consumers, we think we are making informed and conscious decisions about the things we buy, but our unconscious mind is calling all the shots.

WHY YOU NEED A NEW CORVETTE

An example would be automobiles. The purpose of a car is to move us safely and comfortably from point A to point B. Speed limits and traffic conditions dictate just how fast we perform the task of moving from point A to point B. Notwithstanding people's willingness to violate traffic laws, all cars basically accomplish the same task, except for the issues of seating capacity, all-wheel drive, and storage. Yet there are new cars on the market today that sell for under $20,000 and others that are priced in the millions. Now, in reality someone in the market for a million-dollar car is not the same person as the $20,000 buyer. But what about the difference between the $20,000 car and one for $30,000? Or $40,000 and $65,000? Can emotion make a jump in a buying decision of $25,000?

This is where the unconscious mind takes over and emotion controls the buyer's behavior. The unconscious mind starts to relate to how the more expensive car will make the owner feel the prestige of driving that car. The unconscious mind will also note the extra safety features. The unconscious mind will deliver all the data and the reasoning necessary for the conscious mind to make a "good" decision and spend the extra money.

Here is what this looks like: A middle-aged man visits a Chevrolet dealership with the thought of purchasing a new car. He has a price in mind in the $40,000 range, so he is considering a new Camaro, SUV, or pickup truck.

As he walks into the showroom, there on the showroom floor is a brand new, bright red Corvette. He has been watching the television commercials and has seen several online videos that present the car in a very sexy and alluring fashion.

He walks around the car for a minute, admiring the body, the curves of the car, and all the great features. At this moment, his unconscious mind is wanting the car. Our buyer is imagining himself behind the wheel. He is unconsciously dreaming of the looks he will receive when he is driving it. He is experiencing the comments that his friends and coworkers will say to him.

Simultaneously, his conscious mind is telling him it is excessive, it is too much money, and he needs to be more practical. But now the car salesman enters the picture. The first thing he does is what every car salesperson is trained to do—get the customer behind the wheel. He gets our guy in the car and lets him feel the leather-wrapped steering wheel and the racing-type seats. The salesperson then says, "Let's go for a test drive." Our buyer resists, but the salesperson continues to tell him, "It's just for fun. It will only take me a second to grab my dealer plate."

Now, as our buyer is driving the car, he sees himself owning it. The salesperson starts to tell him how the Corvette is the best value in sports cars and how the resale on Corvettes is much higher than on any other American-made car. He explains to the buyer that with the higher resale and the better lease options, this buyer could be driving the new Corvette for only $100 a month more than the cheaper Camaro.

What takes place next is a negotiation between the unconscious and the conscious mind. Our man's unconscious mind is now informing the decision and rationalizing it by the better resale price, the marginal difference in payment, how it could help his status at work, how he can easily save $100 from other expenses he could cut, how he has been working very hard, and how rewarding himself with such a vehicle would be very motivating.

And just like that, the unconscious mind is triggered to drive up a $40,000 purchase into a $65,000 purchase in a matter of minutes.

IV

THINKING PROCESSES/ HEURISTICS

USING HEURISTICS—YOUR TWO BRAINS

Not unlike the comparison of the grape and beach ball is the thinking process comparison developed by Daniel Kahneman. He defines the thinking process as System 1 and System 2.

In his book *Thinking, Fast and Slow* (Kahneman, 2011), Kahneman's central thesis is this dichotomy of thought process of System 1 being fast, intuitive, and emotional, and System 2 being slower, thoughtful, and deliberate.

As just mentioned, System 1 is fast, intuitive, and emotional. An example of a System 1 function would be estimating that an object is closer than another object, while a System 2 function would be parking a car in a tight spot.

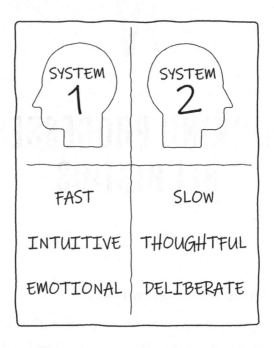

We self-identify with the logical System 2 thinking, when most people are far more System 1 thinkers. System 1 originates first impressions and feelings that are the main source for explicit beliefs and choices of System 2.

System 1 runs automatically while System 2 runs in a comfortable, low-effort mode in the background. When the two systems agree, impressions get turned into beliefs and deliberate choices of System 2. But when System 1 runs into trouble, it asks for the processing power of System 2. Examples of System 2 processing would be deciding between the features of two appliances or calculating 25×114.

This model works well most of the time, except that System 1 has systematic errors due to biases. These biases run the gamut from confirmation bias (only searching for information that agrees with your current belief) to availability bias (depending on the information you hear most frequently as facts). We will discuss the various forms of bias later in this work.

System 2 is basically lazy and does not like to put out much effort. One of its main functions is to monitor and control thoughts and actions suggested by System 1. If we are creating advertising messages that require deep thought or consideration, then we must structure them in a fashion that will engage System 2.

Kahneman explains this using the concept of heuristics.

HEURISTICS: MENTAL SHORTCUTS

Heuristics were first introduced by Kahneman and Amos Tversky in a landmark article called "Judgment under Uncertainty: Heuristics and Biases" (Kahneman & Tversky, 1974).

A heuristic is a mental shortcut, something that allows

humans to come to a conclusion or an answer with minimum effort. Some people would refer to these heuristics as trial and error, guesstimates, rules of thumb, educated guesses, intuitive, profiling, and common sense.

Evolutionary psychology states that humans have evolved to burn the fewest number of calories possible since, in hunter/gatherer days, we did not know when our next meal would be, so Mother Nature designed us to conserve energy.

According to evolutionary anthropologist Doug Boyer of Duke University, our brains, which make up 3 percent of average body mass, use from 20 percent to 25 percent of our total energy just at rest (Boyer, 2018). When we place this fuel-guzzling organ under additional stress, it burns even more.

As a means of conserving energy, our human brains are always looking for a shortcut to relieve us of the necessity of thinking. (One look at Congress should be more than enough evidence to prove how humans avoid thinking!)

These shortcuts are what make up heuristics. Using heuristics in our advertising copy can allow us to avoid critical thinking on the part of the viewer and get them to make a decision without a significant amount of thought at all.

There is power in the word "because." A well-known study by famed Harvard professor Ellen Langer proved this point in 1978. Langer and a team of graduate students set out to prove that to change behavior, humans only needed to know there was a reason to comply with a request, and that the nature of the reason was irrelevant (The Power of Because, 2020).

Langer and her students used the campus copy machine as their testing ground. (For context for younger readers, students used to stand in line to copy papers in a pre-printers and internet age.) Langer had her students request to cut into line at a busy college bookstore copier. The researchers used three different specifically worded scripts when asking to cut in line:

"Excuse me, I have five pages, may I use the copy machine?"

"Excuse me, I have five pages, may I use the copy machine BECAUSE I have to make copies?"

"Excuse me, I have five pages, may I use the copy machine BECAUSE I'm in a rush?"

The first script got a compliance rate of 60 percent. This became the baseline response rate.

The second script, which gave a very weak reason, received a 93 percent compliance rate.

The third script, which gave a legitimate reason, received a compliance of 94 percent. The minor difference of 1 percent demonstrates the power of one word: because.

What Langer's study demonstrated is that it makes no difference what follows the word "because." It can be a ridiculous reason or a legitimate one; it simply does not matter as long as "because" precedes it.

When people hear the word "because," their mind goes on a form of autopilot or heuristic defaulting to the idea that anything that has a reason should be agreed to.

This works especially well with children. You can tell a child to clean their room and get little to no compliance. But if you tell the kid to clean their room "because...," you are likely to get buy-in, even if the "because" is not that relevant. As an example, "You need to clean your room today BECAUSE we are going to dinner tomorrow."

In reality, going out to dinner tomorrow has nothing to do with the condition of the child's bedroom. Again, the reason is not what is important, just the fact that there is one.

In advertising copy, we would use this heuristic as a closing line and call to action.

"Pick up product X today, BECAUSE it works."

"Get brand X mouthwash today, at retailers everywhere, BECAUSE everyone wants fresh breath."

"Find brand X in the snack aisle at your grocery store, BECAUSE it's about time to try something new."

Keep in mind that what happens is when the listener hears the word "because," they become so focused on the transition word and the words that follow that the conscious mind ceases to question the validity of the statement. It allows the command or suggestion that comes before the word "because" to embed in the unconscious mind. That is where all the buying decisions are made.

But there are many other heuristics and biases that play into how humans make decisions. These can also be leveraged in advertising copy to maximize outcomes.

HEURISTICS: PATTERN THINKING—WE ARE ALL LIVING IN A TRANCE

To better explain heuristics, we need to examine pattern thinking. We know in hypnosis and NLP that the human brain is a pattern-recognition machine. We all go from pattern to pattern throughout our day, in the form of a hypnotic state.

An example is your drive to work. When you first get in the car, you do not decide or think about how to start the car. You have a pattern already established for doing this, as well as one for buckling a seat belt, exiting the driveway, and driving to work.

As you are driving to work, you are not thinking about how to get there. Your unconscious mind is doing all of the driving while you talk on the phone, listen to the radio, or contemplate what you need to do when you get to work. Even choosing the exit from the freeway is done at an unconscious level.

Also, your unconscious mind is the superior driver compared to your conscious mind. Here is how: Let us say that while on that drive to work today, a car enters the freeway and immediately swerves into your lane. Without thought, your eyes will check for traffic next to you, swerve into the next lane to avoid the crash, and then recover from the maneuver. Only after the event is completed and you have safely avoided the accident will your conscious mind kick in and analyze what just took place.

Heuristics lean into this pattern-thinking behavior. It is

important to understand how these pattens work and how the use of heuristics interact if we are to take advantage of them for advertising messages.

Kahneman asserts that System 1 thinking involves associating new information with existing patterns, or thoughts, rather than creating new patterns for each experience (Kahneman, 2011).

An example would be in the legal profession. A judge presented with a legal argument will tend to lean into heuristics or previous cases rather than analyze the unique features and issues in the case before them.

Another example of this would be seeing two billboards on the side of a freeway—one advertising a well-known franchise restaurant, the other advertising a local restaurant. Most people will default to the known brand since they have developed a mental shortcut and a bias toward the franchise restaurant, not considering that the local place may be better.

HEURISTICS: ANCHORING EFFECT/CONDITIONING—WHEN DID GANDHI DIE?

The anchoring effect demonstrates our tendency to be influenced by irrelevant numbers. Showing high or low numbers creates high or low responses.

This is the concept to think about when negotiating or developing a price. An example of Kahneman's is the age of Gandhi at his death. In the experiment, some people were asked the question, "Was Gandhi over 140 years old when he died?" These people were then asked to guess at what age he did die (Kahneman, 2011).

The next group was asked, "Was Gandhi over nine when he died?" These people were also asked to guess his age at death. The group exposed to the idea of Gandhi being 140 at death gave a significantly higher guess than the group exposed to the idea of him being nine at his death. This showed that our behavior is far more influenced by our environment at the moment than we would like to believe.

To apply this to advertising and marketing, most people internally guess at the price or the value of a product or service, regardless of the accuracy. Once this number has been established, any number over it will meet with resistance, while a number under it will appear as a value.

Knowing that we are highly influenced by the moment, we can condition a potential buyer to a higher number. An example would be, "10,000 units have been sold for $1,000, but for a limited time, you can own the X product for only $795."

This type of language allows us to establish the higher number, anchoring the consumer to the $1,000 and then appearing to be making a great offer with the lower price.

HEURISTICS: AVAILABILITY

The availability heuristic is a mental shortcut in which people guess at the likelihood or probability of an event based on how easy it is to think of an example. This heuristic operates on the notion that if you can think it, it must be important. In other words, the easier it is to recall the consequences of an action, the greater we perceive these consequences to be.

The availability heuristic shows us that the easier it is to recall the consequences of something, the greater we perceive the consequences to be, even in light of facts to the contrary. As an example, consider the Mega Millions lottery game. We see a 500-million-dollar pot and think of how life-changing winning this would be for us. We then remind ourselves that someone will win it. We then convince ourselves to buy a ticket, even though our chance of winning is 1 in 296 million.

In advertising, we can create these consequences for the consumer in both positive and negative ways. An ad can tell a woman that if she wears a certain perfume, men will pay attention. We can demonstrate this visually without ever saying a single word. On the flip side, we can show what happens to the family who loses the income of a spouse and did not have life insurance to fall back on. By showing visuals of the family losing their home, the car being repossessed, and the family huddled together in panic, we create the feelings of devastation without the viewer ever really experiencing it.

HEURISTICS: SUBSTITUTION/ATTRIBUTION—THREE-CARD MONTE FOR YOUR BRAIN

This is the most famous of all Kahneman and Tversky's experiments. It is based on the idea that humans will replace difficult questions with easier ones. It is the most controversial of all Kahneman's experiments and is commonly referred to as the "Linda problem" (Kahneman, 2011).

Subjects were told a story about Linda, an imaginary young woman. The description: she is single, a student, outspoken, very bright, and concerned with discrimination and social justice.

The subjects were then given two choices: (a) Linda is a bank teller, or (b) Linda is a feminist bank teller. The overwhelming response was that Linda is a feminist bank teller. This answer completely defies logic and probability since all bank tellers are bank tellers, but not all bank tellers are feminists.

The participants dropped the occupation qualifier from the equation and immediately defaulted to the more emotional answer that a young woman interested in social justice would likely be a feminist.

This demonstrates how, by crafting messages that attach more emotionally charged concepts, we can completely override a person's rational thinking process. An example would be the Marlboro man. The visual was a rugged cowboy riding his horse on the open plain, herding cattle, and smoking a Marlboro. The quick attribution that happens is that all cowboys smoke and the manly, rugged ones smoke Marlboro.

HEURISTICS: OPTIMISM AND LOSS AVERSION—THE GLASS IS HALF FULL...EVEN WHEN IT IS NOT

This is referred to as the optimistic bias, which is likely the most important of all the biases. It is how we create the illusion of being in control of our lives.

A simple experiment demonstrates our attraction toward unwarranted optimism. The planning fallacy is the tendency to overestimate benefits and underestimate costs, inducing people to take on risky projects. For example, in 2002, a survey showed that the average American estimated a kitchen remodeling project to be $18,658. However, the real number was $38,769: $18,658 vs. $38,769 (Holt, 2011).

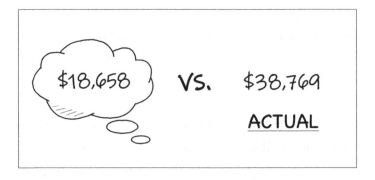

To explain this overconfidence, Kahneman introduced his concept of "what you see is all there is" (WYSIATI) (Kahneman, 2011), which is the theory that when the mind makes decisions, it works from the basis of known knowns.

The issue is that humans tend to reduce or ignore the possibility of known unknowns and that we totally exclude the possibility of unknown unknowns. We tend to fail to take into account the complexity of the world around us. Instead, we lean into our own small and limited understanding of it.

We also tend to ignore the effect that chance can have in our life and instead assume that the outcome will mirror or be similar to some experience that we have had in the past. A perfect example of this is Ikea furniture. We may have assembled a very simple box in the past and thus assume that we can put a larger, more complex piece of furniture together with the same ease.

This is important for advertising immunizations. If we frame our messages around known knowns, we will reduce the consumers' thoughts about known unknowns and create a more familiar and comforting feeling around our offering. As an example, if we were running ads to vacation in the Mexican Riviera, we would show beautiful beaches, large pools, and good-looking people having fun in the sun (optimistic bias). We would skip showing foodborne illnesses, beggars on the streets, and drug gang violence (loss aversion bias).

A group of participants were asked if they would opt for a surgery if the success rate was 90 percent. Meanwhile, another group was asked if they would opt for a surgery if it had a 10 percent failure rate (Kahneman, 2011).

The 90 percent group overwhelmingly voted in favor of the surgery while the 10 percent group did not. This is due to the framing of the question and the way our minds calculate risk. A rational System 2 thinker would realize that these are identical, but a System 1 emotional mind sees the chance of 10 percent failure as a much higher risk.

Another example is the legal position. A prosecutor tells a jury in a murder trial that DNA evidence is 99.9 percent accurate and that the defendant is this 99.9 percent match. To the jury, this is a faceless, dehumanized statistic that appears to be absolute.

When the defense attorney gets to discuss the DNA evidence with the jury, she explains that DNA evidence is used to wrongfully convict 1 out of every 1,000 defendants. She has now created a visual image in the jury's mind of this one person being wrongfully convicted and going to prison for life for a crime he did not commit.

If our defense attorney is really creative, maybe she will tell a story about a real person she knows or represented where the DNA evidence was ultimately found to be wrong.

Logically we know that statistically this defendant most likely committed this crime, especially when combined with other evidence. But due to the framing heuristics of the jurors, there are now 12 people considering if they want to be the person who convicts that 1 in 1,000 innocent man to life in prison. Remember that the jury has been told to find him guilty beyond a reasonable doubt.

You can imagine how dramatic of an effect this has when creating advertising copy. "Ninety percent of guests say they would take their next vacation at our hotels." Conversely, "Only 10 percent of our former guests claim they would not return to our hotels in the future." It is the exact same math equation, but which ad would you respond to?

HEURISTICS: THE SUNK COST FALLACY—WHY THE HOUSE ALWAYS WINS

This is a heuristic that plagues all individuals, even seasoned business professionals. This is due to loss avoidance. As humans, we try to avoid loss whenever we can. We are generally very loss averse. This is why a business is likely to invest more money into a failed project rather than just pull the plug on it and use it as a learning experience. This is the same reason why militaries tend to continue on with battles long after it is obvious who will win. The same holds true for political campaigns.

The movie *The Money Pit* plays into sunk cost fallacy. In the movie, a couple finds what appears to be a great deal on a house (a million-dollar mansion that is available for $200,000, so they buy it. However, once they own the house, problems keep coming to light, including plumbing, electrical, a stairway collapse, and more. This leads the couple to pour more money into it to try to fix it up. While the picture is a comedy and hilarity ensues as they attempt to get the money for the never-ending repairs, the truth is many people find themselves in similar situations with houses.

Additionally, we probably all have either had, or know someone who has had, a car that kept needing repair after repair, but a new car seemed too expensive. We would not want to get rid of a car that we just installed $500 in new tires on, right? This is the epitome of sunk cost fallacy.

Sadly, gamblers also suffer from this. They feel if they can just "win the next one," whether it is the next game, the next hand, or the next spin of the roulette wheel, they will "make up" the losses they have had. It is a vicious cycle of losing, peppered with a few scattered wins here and there, which become the fuel to hang onto hope that never pays off in the end.

Sunk cost fallacy does not only affect individuals. The way this plays out in business too often is that firms double down on bad decisions or bad products instead of cutting losses.

Ford Motor Company did this when they purchased Jaguar and Land Rover. They attempted to incorporate the brands into the Ford brand family, but these types of luxury vehicles were outside their wheelhouse. However, even though they were losing money, they continued to dump additional dollars into trying to make the brands work for them, but it was to no avail.

They ultimately sold Jaguar and Land Rover to Tata for half of what they originally purchased it for. They lost more than 30 billion dollars with all of their doubling down. It was the costliest mistake in Ford's history, even eclipsing the Edsel.

As advertisers, sunk cost fallacy creates opportunities for us. Imagine you are the marketer of an acne treatment. A large portion of your customers do not get the desired response they wanted. You can lean into the sunk cost emotion they have by offering the companion product, the missing piece in the treatment, or drawing people back into the brand by creating compelling content that convinces them they were using it wrong all along.

HEURISTICS: NEGATIVE—YES, I CAN MAKE YOU SQUAWK LIKE A CHICKEN

Sometimes the use of a single word can drastically reduce the response to an ad. This would be the case of negative heuristics.

If you have ever seen a stage hypnotist, you watched as he called up several people from the audience. This is all legit. The people are really selected randomly and are not "plants" as many people suspect.

The hypnotist starts his routine by identifying which people are most susceptible to being hypnotized quickly. (All people can be hypnotized, but on stage you need the ones who will go quickly). He sorts them out by saying:

> "I want you to hold out your hands in front of you, pushing your hands away from your body as hard as you can. Now interlace your fingers and squeeze your hands together so that you can really feel your palms pressing against each other.
>
> Now as you keep pressing them together, I want you to TRY to pull them apart, TRY harder, TRY as hard as you can. No matter how hard you TRY, you cannot get your hands apart."

What happens next is that out of the 20 people who were called on stage, 5 of them did pull their hands apart, but the remaining 15 "magically" had their hands stuck together. The hypnotist will quietly dismiss the 5 who broke and continue the show with the 15 remaining subjects. Note that this is about 75 percent compliance.

Here is why it works. First, by pushing the hands far from the body and interlacing the fingers, the hypnotist has created leverage that works against your hands coming apart.

But the real and major reason it works is because of the word "try." "Try" is a word that has been programmed into our unconscious mind to represent "no." It is our way of excusing ourselves from doing something that we do not really want to do.

Here is an example: It is Thursday afternoon, and you get a call from a friend of a friend. The caller tells you that they are moving into a new apartment on Saturday and they are short on help. They tell you how much they could really use your help.

You as a person do not feel comfortable saying no, but you already have several things planned for the weekend. So, what do you tell the friend? You tell them that you have several things going on, but say, "I will really TRY to come by for a while to help."

You know you are not going to comply with the request,

but using the heuristic "try" word allows you to feel better about yourself. Now you do not have to deal with the confrontation of saying *no*, and *try* allows you to convince yourself that maybe you will find a few minutes to help out.

When you use "try" in advertising copy, you are giving the customer an unconscious signal that they do not need to buy your product. An example of this would be an ad that includes language like, "Try brand X today." The unconscious message is, "You may like this product, but you really do not need to try it."

HEURISTICS: PROSPECT THEORY—THE SIMPLE REASON FOR STOCK MARKET CRASHES

The last heuristic I will discuss is the work that earned Kahneman the Nobel Prize. It is called prospect theory. This is especially important for marketers. Prospect theory demonstrates that economic rationality is not reflected in a person's actual choices. This is due to people's loss aversion and that most people will choose to avoid a loss over getting a gain. In the inverse, people will move toward the loss when the gain reaches a certain emotional point (Kahneman, 2011).

When you give people the option of a 1 percent chance to win $10 versus a 10 percent chance to win $5, they will almost always choose the 10 percent chance. Now when the very same people are given the option of a 45 percent chance to win $10 or a 54 percent chance to win $5, they will choose the 45 percent chance.

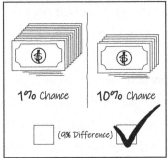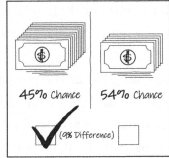

If you examine the mathematics of these two problems, you will see that they are exactly the same amount of risk. However, our minds see 1 percent as impossibly poor odds and we act to avoid the loss. But when we see 45 percent and 54 percent, we see them as relatively equal risk, so we opt for the higher reward. This is in complete opposition to Daniel Bernoulli's Utility Theory. Bernoulli theorized that people would examine opportunities and risks based on a rational set of standards (Bernoulli, 1954).

This concept of prospect theory explains why we experience many stock market dips and crashes. As an example, a common problem seen in the market is when one company in a sector is hit with a lawsuit or maybe a federal investigation. Logic and math tell us that the other companies in the sector are not experiencing these problems and have no change in their business model, profitability, or market share. In spite of this, experienced traders—people who make their living analyzing companies, people who should be immune from emotion—will immediately start to sell off all the other stocks they hold in the same sector over fear that the entire category is going to get hit.

The truth is, when one company in a sector is having problems, this can often mean an increase for the other players as customers may move their business to them. Rationally, no one should sell off. But once the selloff starts, traders find it difficult to not jump on the bandwagon.

While loss avoidance supersedes most people's desire for gain due to emotions, that very same emotion can be pushed to a limit where the effect reverses.

The odds of winning the Mega Millions jackpot are 1 in 302,600,000, and the odds of winning the Powerball lottery are 1 in 292,200,000. The odds of winning both lotteries are 1 in 88 quadrillion; that is the number 88 followed by 15 zeros. To put this in perspective, your odds of being attacked by a shark are 1 in 3,748,067. Your chance of being hit by lightning is 1 in 1,171,000, and the chance of being injured in your own bathroom is 1 out of 10,000.

With all this overwhelming evidence and lack of reasonable odds, you would think that no rational person would ever play the lottery. What is even more bizarre is how the volume of tickets sold skyrockets as the jackpot grows, as if the size of the prize somehow improves the odds of winning.

Why does the fear of loss not kick in here for most people? First, it is people rationalizing illogical decisions with the idea that someone is going to win, and they need a ticket to have a chance. But this is not the real reason. The real motivation is driven by the unconscious mind. What the lottery ticket represents is the permission to dream. As the prize grows in value, we are given permission to dream even bigger.

Every purchase decision that a consumer makes is based on "moving away from" something or "moving toward" something. It is up to us as marketers to craft the messages and use the right language to activate the unconscious emotion in every consumer.

V

WORLD MODELS

Every person has a certain number of filters that they use to interpret the world around them. In Chomsky's 1957 thesis titled *Syntactic Structure*, he theorized that there are three processes that people use to develop these filters: deletion, distortion, and generalization.

DELETION

In his paper of 1956 titled *Seven Plus or Minus Two*, American psychologist George Miller presented the concept that the human mind can only hold seven bits of information at a time, plus or minus two. This is the basis for the grape on top of the dime on top of the beach ball explanation.

Miller's explanation is that on a good day, we can handle up to nine bits of information, and on a bad day we are down to five. He shares that it is as Chomsky argued; we delete the rest of the information coming at us (Miller, 1956).

This is the reason why phone numbers are seven digits. In the 1980s a French telephone company decided to move to an eight-digit phone number in Paris. It turned into a fiasco. People were trying to develop their own internal model to remember phone numbers. For some it was two groups of four, for others it was four groups of two, while others tried to add prefixes before the numbers.

The bottom line is that we take in the information we can hold at the moment and we delete the rest. Imagine how important this thinking is for advertising. Is the message important enough to be recorded, or is it just deleted? A commercial that seems generic and tries to address the needs of everyone is easily forgotten, versus an ad that is very targeted and addresses a very personal or targeted need of a specific group of individuals.

DISTORTION

Chomsky's second model is distortion. We all distort reality; it may be through hallucination or from our own biases. As an example, have you ever walked into an empty room, like a new house or apartment, and imagined what your furniture would look like in the room, or what you could do with the right decorating? This is a hallucination and distortion of reality.

Some distortion that you may have experienced includes firsthand statements that do not add up, or conclusions that someone states that simply do not match the facts. For example: "He never brings me flowers, so he doesn't love me." Logically we can understand that this statement may not be true. Perhaps he does not love the speaker, but it is also possible that he does not have the money, the florist is not on his way, or he simply does not think about flowers as a way to show his love.

Other statements that fit this are ones in which one thing is blamed for causing another: "My kids are driving me crazy." Are your kids literally driving you crazy or does it make more sense to look at what they are doing that you are opting to go crazy?

GENERALIZATION

The third process in the Chomsky model is generalization. Generalization is where you take a few examples or previous experiences and then make a generalization. As an example, when we are young, we learn to open a door. We figure out that when we twist the doorknob, and push or pull on it, the door opens. We then see that we can let go of the doorknob and the door will close again.

After three or four successful times opening doors, our mind builds a generalization of how a door works, and we apply this generalization to every door we see in the future. We can now open and close doors with no thought needed. We do this totally unconsciously. In other words, the beach ball is in charge.

This works until the day we get to a door and there is no knob. Now our conscious mind must go back to work to figure out how this door operates. We will still lean on our previous experiences, but we now need to discover and figure out the new mechanism. These generalizations are how we see the world.

APPLICATION IN ADVERTISING

When we are trying to communicate with consumers, we have to take these three concepts to heart. Is the consumer distorting my message? Are they misunderstanding it? Am I speaking to them in a framework that allows them to misinterpret the message? If my message is being distorted, is it in a negative or positive way?

A positive distortion is that I am selling wrinkle cream, and the consumer starts to distort reality and sees herself looking younger or less wrinkled. She is experiencing the outcome of buying the product prior to even owning it. She is presupposing the outcome.

What if I am selling exercise equipment? Instead of the consumer presupposing how they might look and feel after using it for a month, they instead start to distort or imagine the hard work it takes and how it may be painful or exhausting to do this particular exercise. To overcome the hard work issue, you would show the results of people with great bodies and show them enjoying and having fun doing the exercise.

AVOIDING PAIN OR SEEKING PLEASURE: WHICH IS STRONGER?

Remember that all buying decisions are based on moving away or moving toward. Moving away, or the avoidance of pain, is always more powerful than moving toward pleasure. We never want to raise feelings of moving away from our product. If we are using avoidance of pain as our selling angle, our product needs to clearly demonstrate that we are the solution and the answer to avoidance. Freud argued that all human decision is based on the pleasure principle (Freud, 1895).

When we are talking about advertising, we want to think of avoidance or "move away" language as being reactive and "move toward" language as being proactive. This is because, if we are offering a solution to a problem, the consumer is likely reacting to something, as opposed to moving toward pleasure, which is likely to be proactive.

"Toward" sentence structure should address what they gain, what they want, goals, achievement, or inclusion. Reactive or "toward" language is very specific: "Let's think about it," "Now that you have analyzed it," "Now you really understand," "This is the reason why," "Consider this," "Does this clears it up for you?" "Think about your answer," "You might consider," "The time is right," "Good luck is coming your way."

"Away from" sentence structures should mention situations to be avoided or moved away from, things to avoid, things to get rid of, exclusion of unwanted situations, or problems. Proactive or "away from" language is very different, but equally specific: "Go for it," "Just do it," "Jump in," "Why wait?" "Now," "Right away," "Get it done," "You can do it," "You'll get to do X," "Take charge," "Take the initiative," "Run away with it," "Right now," "What are you waiting for?" and "Let's hurry."

PROACTIVE
PLEASURE

REACTIVE
PAIN

Although reactive and proactive can be personality types based on the NLP Meta models, when it comes to marketing and advertising, consumers can switch back and forth between them and at times even experience both simultaneously. As an example, most medicinal products are "moving away" from, such as aches and pains, infections, etc. Although it is certainly desirable to not be in pain, it is not something we interpret as an upgrade as much as it is returning to normal or homeostasis. In contrast, the desire for a designer handbag, luxury car, or even a bag of potato chips would be focused on the pleasure side of the theory.

When selling beauty products, we are primarily working within a reactive mode. There could be some desire to avoid looking older, but the real driver is the distortion view of what the user will look like after using the product.

A consumer considering a new car could have equal reactive and proactive motivations. On the reactive, they could be experiencing breakdowns with their current car. Maybe they have been stranded with it or had to continually invest in repairs. In the meantime, they can be proactive, imagining how they will feel in the new car, and how it will make them appear to others.

It is important to observe cultures when marketing to professions. Some professions have "away from" or "toward" cultures inherent in their business. As an example, consider the medical profession. Although there are doctors today practicing functional and preventive medicine, this is not the norm. The typical doctor is looking for symptoms and devising treatment to "move away" from the illness. So, as an example, if we were selling the drug Nuvigil, we would not promote to a doctor that it can increase human performance or raise IQ in some patients. We would promote that it works to keep patients suffering with narcolepsy awake and functional.

What if we are selling quantitative software to stockbrokers? We would not spend nearly as much time promoting the algorithms' ability to limit downside risk as we would discussing how using it can lead to above-average gains for the broker and their customers. For the stockbroker, not losing the client's money is the cost of entry; making the client money is how you keep the client and get more of their investment dollars.

VI

METAPHORS

THE FATHER OF HYPNOTHERAPY

No discussion of hypnosis or neuro-linguistic programming (NLP) can be complete without discussing Dr. Milton Erickson. Erickson was an American psychiatrist and the father of modern hypnotherapy. Although Erickson was the leader in hypnosis, he only used formal hypnosis in one-fifth of his sessions (*BT10 Fundamentals of Hypnosis 04*, 2010). The real unique skill of Erickson was his use of metaphors.

Erickson understood and mastered the premise that anything that assumes trance causes trance. In other words, you do not have to formally induce someone into a trance state in order to deliver unconscious commands or information.

The Wikipedia page on Erickson (Wikipedia, 2020) sums up how well he used this metaphor model:

Erickson believed that the unconscious mind was always listening and that, whether or not the patient was in trance, suggestions could be made which would have a hypnotic influence, as long as those suggestions found resonance at the unconscious level. The patient could be aware of this or could be completely oblivious that something was happening. Erickson would see if the patient would respond to one or another kind of indirect suggestion and allow the unconscious mind to participate actively in the therapeutic process. In this way, what seemed like a normal conversation might induce trance, or a therapeutic change in the subject.

The basic principle that Erickson subscribed to is that what assumes trance causes trance (*BT10 Fundamentals of Hypnosis 04*, 2010).

Erickson maintained that trance is a common, everyday occurrence. For an example, while waiting for buses or trains, reading or listening or being involved in strenuous exercise, it is quite normal to become immersed in the activity and go into a trance state, removed from any other irrelevant stimuli. These states are so common and familiar that most people do not consciously recognize them as hypnotic phenomena.

The same situation is in evidence in everyday life, however, whenever attention is fixated with a question or an experience of the amazing, the unusual, or anything that holds a person's interest. At such moments people experience the common everyday trance.

Because Erickson expected trance states to occur naturally and frequently, he was prepared to exploit them therapeutically, even when the patient was not present with him in the consulting room. This would be similar to how we are not present with a consumer when they encounter an advertising message. He also discovered many techniques for increasing the likelihood that a trance state would occur. He developed both verbal and nonverbal techniques and pioneered the idea that the common experiences of wonderment, engrossment, and confusion are, in fact, just kinds of trance. We will explore these later in this work.

Clearly, there are a great many kinds of trance. Many people are familiar with the idea of a "deep" trance. Earlier in his career, Erickson was a pioneer in researching the unique and remarkable phenomena that are associated with that state, spending many hours at a time with individual test subjects, deepening the trance.

That a trance may be "light" or "deep" suggests a one-dimensional continuum of trance depth, but Erickson would often work with multiple trances in the same patient—for example, suggesting that the hypnotized patient behave "as if awake," thereby blurring the line between the hypnotic and awake state.

Erickson's belief that there are multiple states that may be utilized resonates with Charles Tart's idea, put forward in the book *Waking Up* (Tart, 2001) that all states of consciousness are trances and that what we call "normal" waking consciousness is just a "consensus trance." NLP also makes central use of the idea of changing state, without it explicitly being a hypnotic phenomenon.

We are all in constant states of trance throughout our day, and many times we move from one trance state to another one. Being involved in a movie or watching a sporting event is trace state. Think of the emotional and sometimes illogical responses, such as yelling at a player or an official through a television or wearing a lucky hat or shirt to watch the game, that people have at sporting events or even watching them on television. It is because of the trance state that the viewer has entered.

Trance is simply a time of extemporaneous focus. Think about the last time you attended a great movie. As you became deeper and deeper involved in the movie, outside stimuli drifted off and your peripheral vision narrowed. You stopped noticing the other people sitting in the theater with you. You disconnected from noticing the temperature of the room. This trance state is created by the power of great storytelling.

Erickson was a master storyteller. His patients would

become enthralled with his detailed and colorful stories, while the entire time Erickson was delivering both direct and indirect instructions to their unconscious minds.

Many of Erickson's patients would feel and get better within a single session but had no idea why it happened, since it was done at such a subliminal level that their conscious mind was not aware that it took place (*BT10 Fundamentals of Hypnosis 04*, 2010). Erickson understood that in addition to strong rapport, the more prestige and credibility he developed, the more authority and command he would have over his subjects.

One example of this was a case where the parents of a young man sent him to see Dr. Erickson regarding his use of marijuana. Erickson asked the young man if he smoked pot. The young man answered, "Yes." Erickson went on to ask him if he could quit; the young man again said, "Yes." Erickson then said, "Stop it. And now go home and leave my office." It is reported that the boy did stop using the drug and the parents were happy with the outcome (*BT10 Fundamentals of Hypnosis 04*, 2010).

For marketers, an example of how a brand can build authority over their consumer base is what Apple has done. People will stand in line for the latest iPhone, even though the differences could be nearly indistinguishable from what they already own.

An Ericksonian metaphor is the result of an interaction between two different domains—in other words, something being similar to or reminiscent of. As humans, we live in a metaphorical state and it is nearly impossible for us to communicate without the use of metaphors. Examples include, "I feel pumped over that movie," "That really drives your point," and "That last exam was a walk in the park."

No one actually attaches themselves to a pump during a movie, drives points at anything, or walks in a park while taking an exam. These are simply metaphors that allow us to place language and an event into context.

Music is also a metaphor. While the melody or sound can help place us into a trance state, the lyrics can deliver many deep meanings at an emotional level through indirect messages. Think back to music of your youth. When you hear a specific song, it can take you back in time. Think about how songs can become representative of a relationship or a feeling that you have for another person, like how couples often have "their" song.

Music as metaphor is used to drive certain feelings or themes in movies. As an example, consider the song "Eye of the Tiger" in the *Rocky* movies. The beat and style of the song is a hard-driving, pulse-lifting cadence, while the lyrics use the metaphor of a tiger to drive the high emotional charge in the scenes it is attached to.

In visual forms of advertising, metaphors are created by merging two seemingly unrelated images or concepts together in an effort to create symbolism. Metaphors can be used to reinforce the value of the product or to make it seem more personal. They can also be used to create a specific brand image. An advertising metaphor often combines a verbal phrase with a visual image to enforce the dramatic effect.

Armed with all this information, imagine if you could create advertising messages that have such deep resonating meaning far beyond the consumers' conscious mind. Erickson has given us that road map with his explanation of using metaphors.

Tropicana orange juice used the metaphor that their juice is "what sunshine tastes like." Think of the multiple meanings that your unconscious mind can derive from this: the sun is bright and feels good, the sun is natural and healthy, Tropicana is grown in sunlight, not manmade. All of these meanings and more can be transferred to the product in the consumer's mind, without the consumer understanding why.

Another example would be Disneyland making the self-proclamation of being "The Happiest Place on Earth." This statement sends the mind on a search for a description or example of what the happiest place on earth must be like.

RAPPORT—HE REALLY LIKES ME

Another concept, and gift if you will, from Erickson was the understanding of rapport. Rapport is an English word derived from the French verb *rapporter*, meaning to bring back to harmony, accord, affinity, and generally ease of understanding, all which are important for good communications.

Rapport is basically a social construct that we all use frequently. In our social lives, we are in rapport with our friends, family, significant other, and people we are attracted to. Just sit in any bar and you will find people going in and out of rapport. You will even find people drifting into rapport to a point of mirroring each other's behavior. One person will cross their legs and then you can see the person they are in rapport with do the same.

You have probably spotted people who are in love; you will find that these people are in such deep levels of rapport that they can finish each other's sentences. These couples will even know when the other is out of sorts or not feeling right. Conversely you can instantly tell when two people are not in rapport. The tension is nearly like an electrical charge in the room.

Rapport means deliberately using social mirroring of images, gestures, nonverbal cues, and language. This allows for anyone, including an advertiser, to quickly get into rapport. We learn about the world via our senses, and we develop an internal model of it and how we relate to it.

We segment our world into categories and learn what we prefer including language, food, music, people, etc. Understanding rapport begins with the knowledge that we all have our own unique model of the world that we keep hidden from others.

Take a moment and think about your favorite meal. Visualize it, see it from every angle, and smell the aroma of it. Maybe it has side dishes next to it or even your favorite dessert is there. Now put the entire meal under a spotlight. Imagine it is bright and colorful and make the image as intense as possible.

If you have really done this exercise, right now you have a very clear picture of your favorite meal. Chances are it is a culmination of memories and experiences that you have assembled to create this perfect image.

Now while my favorite meal may include prime rib cooked rare and a piece of carrot cake, yours is likely to be completely different. However, I promise that as you just read the words of what my favorite meal is, you said to yourself, "Not me. Mine isn't like that." You spotted the words on the page about my favorite and immediately compared it to the mental image of your favorite. You may even have felt slight irritation or discomfort. Or it could be you felt a twinge of pleasure noting how superior your choices are to mine.

Building rapport in advertising is our effort to understand our consumer's model of the world and demonstrate that we share their values. If we want to be in rapport, we need to set our favorite meal aside and be in the other person's meal.

A company that really knows how to be in rapport is Harley-Davidson. If you have spent any time riding motorcycles or even paying attention to motorcycle riders, you will realize that the Harley owner is unique. The bikes tend to be big and loud, and the riders have a common look and manner of dressing.

When walking into a Harley-Davidson dealership, the average Harley owner immediately feels at home, in rapport, and as if they are with their tribe. You will see that the Harley employees are also riders. They share the love of the open road and the Harley experience. The staff is also friendly, welcoming, and on a first-name basis. You will also see that they are dressed like riders.

Because of this instant rapport, the customer feels at home and safe, and more importantly, they feel they can take the advice of these Harley employees when it comes to buying new bikes, parts, accessories, or suggested service. There is little resistance to nearly anything the Harley salesperson may say.

As advertisers, it is important that we get in rapport with our consumer. There are various tools we can use to accomplish this. Do the people seen in our communications appear to be similar to how our consumer envisions themselves? Do we share an ethos with our customer, such as a social cause or charity? If we are marketing to military veterans, we would show other veterans or active-duty personnel in various settings. If marketing to mothers with kids, they will likely respond best to seeing moms like them in familiar settings or scenarios.

Another way to get to rapport is to embrace the consumer's style of language. Is there a regional or urban tone to our consumer language? Is there a gender or generational spin we need to adapt? Do our consumers prefer a certain sarcastic tone to their communications? The use of a celebrity can work here if that celebrity shares some type of values or ethos with our consumer.

Without the creation of rapport, any attempt to communicate or market to any consumer will be suspect and deliver suboptimal results.

METAPHORS: TRANSDERIVATIONAL SEARCH—SENDING YOUR BRAIN ON A SCAVENGER HUNT

The concept to keep in mind when using metaphors in advertising is transderivational search. The process of going back through our world model and searching for experiences that validate new input is called transderivational search. It is what makes an indirect metaphor work.

Referring to Chomsky, we know that we all follow a practice of delete, distort, and generalize. This process helps us develop our own unique view of the world. It is with this model that all our incoming information is correlated and compared. We examine the input both consciously and unconsciously and decide what information fits within our framework or truths and what does not.

To make sense of a metaphor, your mind must go back through the memory banks of past experiences. Once we identify the part that makes sense, we can then accept the data as factual.

While indirect metaphors, such as orange juice tasting "like sunshine," are powerful, there are also direct metaphors that can be used. A direct metaphor is when you develop or create a story line that has the viewer enthralled in a quick, trance-like state. While the metaphor is coming into focus, you give the subject a direct command.

In our orange juice example, we could combine the indirect with the direct: "You will know what sunshine tastes like when you **buy Tropicana orange juice today** at your favorite grocery store." By combining these two techniques, we have caused what is called an embedded command.

Erickson would often create metaphors within metaphors to induce the subject into a deep trance state. Once these metaphors were looped together, he would deliver the direct message to the unconscious mind that would effect the change that the subject needed (*BT06 Dialog 02, Metaphor*, 2006).

As in the Tropicana example above, we are creating a feeling or thought that forces the viewer to go into transderivational search. As the mind is preoccupied with this effort, we insert the direct command, which is to go "buy Tropicana orange juice today."

Returning to the grape and beach ball analogy, think of the grape, the conscious mind, as a spam filter protecting the unconscious mind from anyone trying to influence it. When we create a trance state or force a transderivational search, we shut down the conscious mind, shutting off this spam filter, and we deliver our message directly to the unconscious mind. This is the place where buying decisions are made. It is because it is the unconscious mind that has the massive capacity, not the conscious mind.

One thought that should not be missed here is voice modulation. Although the line about orange juice tasting like sunshine would be voiced in a very melodic and comforting style, to relax the conscious mind and lower defenses, the words "buy Tropicana orange juice today" would be delivered as if it was a direct order. The reason is due to literal communication.

If I ask you, "Do you know your name?" you are likely to say your name. This is because your conscious mind interprets the meanings of words by combining the context, tonality, and body language into the intended meaning.

When we communicate with the unconscious mind, it is completely literal. If I were to ask a person under a hypnotic trance, "Do you know your name?" their answer would be one word: "yes."

Knowing that we induced a quick and mixed trance and forced a transderivational search, we must speak directly to the unconscious mind in very unambiguous terms. That is the reason for the voice modulation.

METAPHORS: USES IN ADVERTISING

There are many ways and types of metaphors that can be used in advertising. The following are some examples and descriptions.

VISUAL METAPHOR

The visual metaphor is useful for communicating a product's benefit by comparing it to something that is different but is built with similar value.

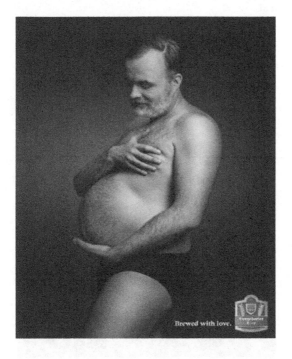

Brewed with love.

In this case, the advertiser, Bergedorfer Bier, is trying to relay that they brew beer with the same care and concern as birthing a child. There is the second, even hidden, metaphor that they are birthing a new beer into the world. By using a man who appears pregnant, the ad gains additional attention because it is disruptive to our minds. A pregnant man?

VISUAL SIMILE

The visual simile is like the visual metaphor as it takes two different things and compares them. However, the difference is that in a simile, the second item is visually similar to the first.

The new Beetle Denim has arrived.

In this ad, Volkswagen is promoting their denim Beetle interior, but the simile is that the stitching looks like the dotted lines of a highway.

In this model, a story is told with visual images, while underpinning it with even deeper, unconscious meaning.

This ad for *Save the Children* shows how the violence in a child's life is destructive, but the underlying message is that each of these traumatic events is like a seed being sown into their heart.

ANALOGIES

Just like word analogies, visual analogies compare two things that, on the surface, appear to be unrelated.

In the case of this ad for the WWF, the analogy is that the ecosystem is like a game of Jenga where, if you remove one piece, the entire system can collapse.

NEGATIVE DRAMATIZATION

The fear of consequence of not using a product has always been a popular metaphor.

In the case of this product, Acnes Treatment Series, we are seeing that the person is feeling shame over her skin condition, yet the solution is right in front of her.

The secondary metaphor being used here is that her acne is preventing her from finding love, as you see the figure of the man holding flowers for her.

Editing software like Photoshop has made this type of metaphor far more popular. What is happening here is the use of a disruptive image, forcing the viewer to search internally (transderivational search) to make sense of the image.

AN OPEN BUCKLE HELMET ISN'T A HELMET.

The metaphor here is that not buckling a helmet is like not having one on.

MINIMALISM

This is communicating with the least number of elements possible.

The image shows the popular Tic Tac as the shape of the open lips. The hidden metaphor is that Tic Tacs are the key to being kissing-ready at a moment's notice.

CONTRAST

The message from Ikea here is clear.

Shopping at Ikea is the way to make you stand out from the crowd and decorate your home in a unique and noticeable style.

Also, compared to the drab gray neighbors, it implies that you and your place will be more fun.

TYPOGRAPHY

This is a form of a visual simile where you use the typography to appear like the object being promoted.

In this case we see that the LG robotic vacuum not only cleans up messes on the floor, but the copy itself is a metaphor that the product helps end domestic arguments over housework.

VISUAL PUNS

Visual puns are good for a quick laugh while still driving the message.

In the case of 2 GINGERS Irish Whisky, the gag is the two redheaded women on some rocks, while driving the message that 2 GINGERS Irish Whisky is sexy and desirable "on the rocks."

DOUBLE MEANING

This metaphor can also be good for a quick laugh like this double meaning ad for Volkswagen.

No need to look back.
Volkswagen with Rear View Camera.

Das Auto.

Not only is the image of someone wearing clothes from a past fashion era, but also that you do not need to look backward when you have a built-in rear camera and that looking back can be embarrassing and uncomfortable.

VISUAL HYPERBOLE

In this ad for Nikon's COOLPIX camera, they have used an extreme hyperbolic example.

The metaphor is that when you take a selfie with a COOLPIX camera, it is as if you have a professional, flying camera crew with you all the time, helping you get the best possible shots.

REVEAL

While at first you just see a bunch of letters, most people will strive to make sense of them. By using the contrasting colors, most people first see the word email, then find the word "girl."

YOU CAN'T SEE BOTH AT THE SAME TIME

TriHonda

The message is that you cannot see both words at once.

The underlying metaphor is you cannot see two things at the same time, so you should stay safe by not driving while texting or emailing.

Combining contrasting images can be used to drive a point and to be disruptive in order to get the viewer's attention.

By swapping or morphing the two people's faces on each other, we see that it really can work, again demonstrating how people are more alike than different.

The underlying metaphor in this ad from National Geographic is that even when there are obvious visual differences, as human beings we are really not that much different from each other.

The technique here is to compare two similar items.

In this case, the comparison was between the two versions of The Scarlet Letter: the movie versus the book.

The underlying metaphor is that books are better than movies, as the movie has a lower rating than the book.

KILLER FACTS

Sometimes shocking headlines with metaphoric imagery are all you need to drive a point.

In this ad, we see a human lying on a bench with a "Hungry" sign and a bag, clearly indicating they are homeless. The person is dressed up like a dog, which does not initially make sense until we read the caption that shares the amount of money spent on pets versus the homeless. It is then we see the dramatic difference in how we spend more money taking care of our dogs than we do the homeless.

This is an example of a well-known symbol driving the point.

The message being conveyed here is that Play-Doh does not involve a computer.

The hidden metaphor is that kids need to spend less time with computers and more time in the physical world. The second metaphor is to remind us of a time when we played with the toy.

With borrowed interest, we leverage the interest of one asset to another, unrelated asset.

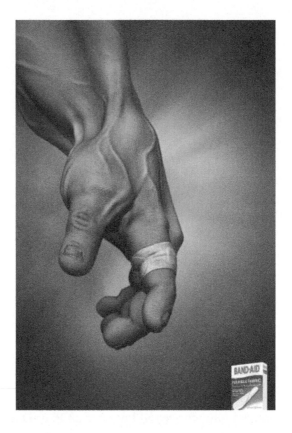

This is a great example of a brand leveraging the popularity of a cartoon character, the Hulk, in pop culture. The underlying metaphor is that Band-Aid must be extremely flexible and strong enough to last on a superhero.

UNCONVENTIONAL IMAGERY

Using odd or unconventional imagery can be effective in capturing attention.

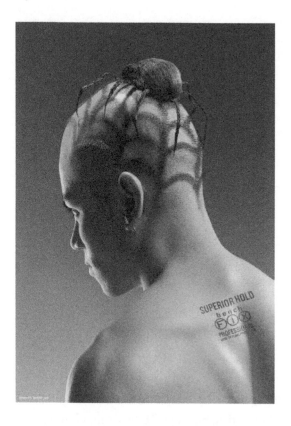

This is especially true for younger consumers. The hidden metaphor is that this BENCH/ product does not conform to traditional values and has an ethos with the unconventional consumer.

CONSEQUENCES

In this ad we see some symbolism that requires the reader to take a moment to figure it out.

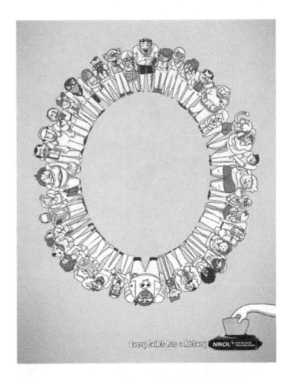

By lining up all these different people in the shape of a toilet seat and inserting the copy "Every toilet has a history," the viewer is capable of realizing that when they use a public toilet, they are coming into contact with hundreds of other people. The message is that you need to sterilize the toilet seat.

VII

PGO SPIKES

CREATING YOUR ONE SHOT

First, let us take a moment to understand what "PGO Spike" means before we get to how it applies to advertising. PGO stands for Ponto-Geniculo-Occipital waves. When we cause these spikes by disrupting patterns, we get a momentary opportunity to connect directly with the unconscious mind.

These waves begin from the pons part of the brain, then move to the lateral geniculate nucleus (LGN), and then to the primary visual cortex of the occipital lobe. Although these waves are the most prominent right before REM sleep begins, they are also present during rapid eye movements in both awake and sleeping subjects.

By leveraging PGO spikes, we can cause momentary periods of brief hypnotic trance, and it is during this trance that we can deliver the instructions, such as why and how to acquire a particular product or service. This is similar to instruction in therapy, where we install the behavior or change work that we want the subject to act upon.

The PGO spike was first demonstrated by Dr. Milton Erickson. Erickson would do something he referred to as a handshake induction. He would reach out to shake a person's hand and would suddenly change the expected experience. For instance, he might lightly brush their palm or reach for their wrist and move their hand to their face (*BT10 Fundamentals of Hypnosis 04*, 2010).

This change in expected experience causes an immediate PGO spike since the conscious mind is knocked offline. A handshake only has a beginning and end, there is no middle, and it is an automatic response. When you insert a middle process or event, the mind has no idea what to do with it.

The purpose behind any trance state is to take the conscious mind offline, shut down the built-in spam filter, and have an open communication to the unconscious mind.

We live our lives following a set of patterns for how we experience the world. The older we get, the more patterns we have developed due to increased experience. When we experience a break or a disruption in one of our patterns, our mind fires off a PGO spike. This then sets us in a moment of hypnosis or trance, when time suspends or distorts, and our thinking becomes unemotional and widespread. When this happens, our prefrontal cortex goes offline, which takes with it our executive function. Now we can access our entire brain and capacity. When this happens for longer periods of time, it is referred to as flow state.

If you were standing on the top of a 10-foot ladder and suddenly fell, but instead of hitting the floor you were just suspended in midair, you would have a PGO spike, because your frame of reference for how the world around you works—gravity—was just broken.

CRASHING A MOTORCYCLE (NOT RECOMMENDED)

Let me give you a personal example. Early one Sunday morning, I was out riding motorcycles with a friend. We were in a rural area where there is normally very little traffic on a Sunday morning. I was heading down a bridge that had orange construction barrels dividing the traffic lanes. As I approached the end of the barrels, I noticed a man driving an SUV in the next lane about 40 feet in front of me.

My frame of reference was that he would see me, as I could see him, and he would stay in his lane. But being cautious, I was prepared for him to merge into my lane with the need to slow down, if necessary. However, he did none of these things. Instead, he made a hard U-turn in front of me the moment his truck cleared the barrels. Once he noticed my large motorcycle headed for his driver's door, he froze and stopped in the center of the road, blocking all possible escape routes.

Although the actual time elapsed was a second or less, it felt like minutes for me. My mind immediately had a PGO spike, knocking the prefrontal cortex offline. I was neither afraid nor emotional; I was only analytical.

My first thought was to evaluate the crash potential. I decided that hitting the truck broadside was not an option as my mind reminded me that hitting cars broadside usually results in rider death. My mind then decided that I needed to put the bike on the ground: to lay it down. I immediately hit the back brake and skidded the bike to the ground on the left side (my dominant side).

Now that the bike was on its side, my brain said that I needed to get away from the vehicle since I could still crash. My mind told me to push off the bike and to hit the ground now, allowing the bike to strike the truck without me. As the bike crashed into the SUV, I slid across the highway spinning and bouncing. Once I came to a stop, I managed to look all around me for oncoming traffic to make sure that I was not going to be run over.

This entire series of decisions happened inside of a second's time, and yet to me it felt like two or three minutes of time. To demonstrate this point even further, look and see how long it takes me to describe the event. In other words, for that moment I was in a hypnotic trance. This trance was created externally, instantly, and it was not within my control.

The point of all this is that PGO spikes are incredibly powerful events that can tap into the brain's deep abilities. While not life and death, we can create PGO spikes in people's minds via advertising. During the brief moment when that trance is induced, we have an open channel to the consumer's unconscious mind. It is during this moment when the selling can take place.

PGO SPIKES: CREATING THE SPIKE

How do we create a PGO spike? We do it through disruption. A PGO spike is created when we disrupt a person's framework of how the world works. This happens when we cause the person to momentarily rethink what they know about the world around them. This spike is created by disrupting or hijacking their thought process.

Here is an example of how to do this in a one-on-one situation. Imagine you are involved with a person who is irate or maybe even angry. This person is on a tirade, going off about whatever has upset them. They are really in the flow of the problem. As they are firing all of this information at you, you simply interject into the conversation that tomorrow you tried to put your shoes on your elbows, but no matter how many times you tried to do it, they just did not fit right.

You have just caused a PGO spike in this person. They will completely stop talking, as their mind has been hijacked, to figure out what you said. But no matter how hard their mind searches for a past experience to put this comment into context, they cannot find it.

What happens next is confusion followed by a question of, "What did you say?" or a statement of, "That didn't make sense." During the brief opening, you interject the comment, "None of this is worth being upset about."

You wait a moment and then ask the subject, "Tell me again why you are so upset?" The subject has now lost their train of thought and is no longer upset. You have defused the argument and programmed their unconscious mind to the thought that this is not worth being upset over.

This is yet another example of how we can use NLP and hypnotic techniques to improve our communications.

PGO SPIKES: PRIVILEGED MOMENTS

While a PGO spike can be used to diffuse situations as demonstrated above, it is only one part of using NLP in advertising. The second part is getting the brain to accept the message that follows.

To do this, we must employ what Robert Cialdini refers to in his bestseller book *Pre-Suasion* as "privileged moments." Cialdini defines a privileged moment as that short, ever-so-slight period of time between when the PGO spike fires and when the subject returns to baseline (Cialdini, 2016).

It is in the split second of confusion that we have the ability to change the narrative or to put our subject on a completely different path.

A demonstration of this occurred during the presidential debates of 2016 when Fox News anchor Megyn Kelly confronted Donald Trump about calling women "pigs" and "dogs." The former president, a master of NLP, followed a textbook PGO spike pattern and performed it on the entire nation. The exchange was as follows:

Kelly: "Mr. Trump, isn't it true that you have called women pigs and dogs?"

Trump: "Yes, I did. But only Rosie O'Donnell."

Notice what Trump did. He said, "Yes, I did." This is not the answer the nation expected to hear from a politician. The typical response would have been, "Megyn, my comments were taken out of context."

By saying, "Yes, I did," he caused a PGO spike in every viewer's mind. Every person said to themselves, "What did he just say?" Then, without pause, he said, "But only about Rosie O'Donnell," creating an image in many viewers' minds, and that his voters agreed with, of a terribly angry and bitter woman.

But Kelly continued to push Trump on the issue:

Kelly: "Haven't you said this about other women?"

Trump instantly responded by pointing a finger at Kelly, to diminish her stature, and called her by her first name to take her down further:

Trump: "Check your facts, Megyn. Check your facts."

With viewers just coming off a PGO spike, and many voters liking what he had delivered, he now positioned Megyn Kelly as a sloppy reporter who did not check her facts. He was able to use NLP and PGO spikes to direct people's thought processes.

PGO SPIKES: USES IN ADVERTISING—INTERRUPTING YOUR AUDIENCE'S WORLDVIEW

We can both cause, and effectively use, PGO spikes in our advertising copy and visuals. Advertisers can deploy the PGO spike model by first interrupting the consumer's worldview and then delivering a powerful message in the split-second "privileged moment." Examples to induce the spike would include disruptive messages such as:

"You should never buy our product...unless you are prepared for a dramatic change."

"Product X is the most expensive X you can buy...because it is worth it."

VISUAL ASPECTS

Another way to disrupt the consumer and cause a PGO spike is with the visual aspects of an ad. As an example, the following ad by Patagonia tells the consumer not to buy a product.

Seeing this causes the consumer to conduct a transderivational search in their mind, looking for information that will make sense out of what the eye is seeing. By forcing the search and the question, Patagonia draws the reader deeper into the ad copy where the real message is delivered.

PRESUPPOSING—"SENATOR, ARE YOU STILL BEATING YOUR WIFE?"

Presuppositions are a common technique used in hypnosis and can be used equally as well in advertising. A presupposition falls into the category of stealth hypnosis and is used to imbed thoughts, ideas, or even direct commands into a person's unconscious mind without their knowledge. You can also stack presuppositions together to overwhelm the conscious mind and break down a person's resistance to your comments.

A presupposition is a structure of language that makes unverbalized assumptions. An example would be, "I am not going to fly to California anymore." This statement assumes that I have flown on an airplane in the past and that I have been to California. Our unconscious mind tends to accept the statements as truths, since our attention has been distracted. In this case, the mind is focused on the idea that I am not going to do this any longer and forgets to question if I have ever (a) been on a plane or (b) been to the state of California.

Another common presupposition is the infamous, "Senator, are you still beating your wife?" In this case, the voter does not question if he is a senator or if he beats his wife. Instead, the focus is on the person and that he used to beat his wife and wondering if he has stopped doing so now.

Presuppositions are part of the Meta Model of NLP and come directly from the work of Dr. Milton Erickson. Erickson used presuppositions on a regular basis. Many times, he was able to affect change in a patient's behavior within minutes and without formally inducing a hypnotic trance state (*BT10 Fundamentals of Hypnosis 04*, 2010).

One famous Erickson story involves a patient who came to him for help with smoking cessation. Erickson knew that he had solved the man's smoking problem with one sentence. He asked the man, "How surprised will you be when you wake up tomorrow as a nonsmoker?"

The man answered, "I'll be very surprised."

The patient did indeed quit smoking the following day. The reason is that he did not question if he would stop smoking. His comment was that he would be very surprised. In other words, he accepted the presupposition as a fact that he was no longer a smoker.

As a marketer, the way to have a similar result is to utilize the Mandel Triangle (Mandel, 2020).

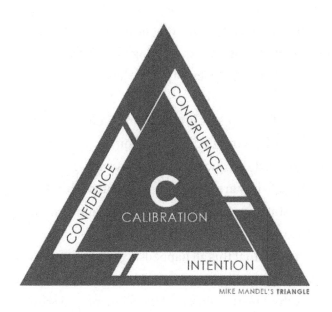

MIKE MANDEL'S **TRIANGLE**

This represents what the therapist needs to have when working with a subject, which also works for marketers— three equal sides or parts: confidence, congruence, and intention in the delivery of your message. In the middle is calibration, which means paying attention to your subject or demographic.

McDonald's restaurants have a long and successful history of using NLP and hypnotic language or even a hypnotic background, such as the sound effects of people eating and enjoying the food, to sell their products. McDonald's has a practice of putting NLP presuppositions right on their packaging.

One such use is the phrase that is printed on the inside lid of some of the Big Mac packaging. The inside cover says, "Unique? You might even say it's delicious."

By asking if the Big Mac is unique and then answering it for you, they trick your unconscious mind into thinking that you answered the question. Next, by saying, "You might even say...," they are imbedding a presupposition that this is a true statement and that you are actually thinking this.

Keep in mind that this all happens right when you open the container of the Big Mac that you have already purchased. So, play this into the context of the moment: you are hungry, you made McDonald's your choice, and you are about to have your first bite. Remember that oftentimes the dream of what you are about to experience exceeds the reality. What McDonald's has done in this case is to presuppose your first bite experience and to set the stage for it being wonderful, regardless of the reality.

AWARENESS—THE POLKA-DOTTED ELEPHANT IN THE ROOM

Anytime you call attention to something or draw awareness to it, you are making it the object of focus. If I say to you, "Do not think about polka-dotted elephants," you immediately see a polka-dotted elephant in your mind. We are not capable of unseeing what is being drawn into our immediate attention and focus.

"Your family will love your vacation to Disney World." Now your attention is drawn to your family loving Disney World. There is no question of wanting to go to Disney World or should you go; it has been replaced by you thinking or imagining how much fun your family will have there. There is no yes or no question to be answered, only an estimation of the amount of fun you will experience.

TIME SEQUENCE—DITCH THE FORMALITIES

You can use time sequencing as a tool to transport a consumer's mind away from asking themselves if they want something to focusing on how long it may take.

When you hear that "SmartMouth mouthwash gives you fresh breath for 12 hours," you completely skip questioning if SmartMouth can really provide fresh breath. Instead, you focus on deciding if it really lasts 12 hours. So, you have already presupposed that it works. The only thing left for you to do is to experience the product and see that it lasts for 12 hours.

"Fungicure treats toenail fungus in as little as four weeks." Again, your mind has completely skipped over the question of whether Fungicure even works and instead gone to questioning if it can really work in four weeks?

If we can get the consumer to recognize and presuppose

that Fungicure indeed does treat toenail fungus, then the only issue standing between us and the sale is the consumer's willingness to find out how fast it works.

THE DOUBLE BIND—WE CAN DO THIS MY WAY, OR MY WAY

The double-bind technique is yet another form of presupposition originally developed by Milton Erickson. What Erickson did was presuppose that the patient was going to follow one of two paths presented. By configuring the statement in such a way that it could not be answered as a yes or no, Erickson got the patient to agree to make the behavioral change that the patient was seeking.

Some examples:

> "Would you like to sit in my hypnosis chair or in my trance chair?"

Either choice presupposes that the subject is going to go into a hypnotic trance once they sit down. No matter which chair the subject picks, they "choose" to be hypnotized.

> "Are you going to tell your family you quit smoking tonight, or will you tell them tomorrow?"

Either way, the subject has already agreed that they have already quit smoking.

Another technique used by Dr. Mike Mandel in his *Architecture of Hypnosis System* (Mandel, 2020) is to look at the subject with a blank stare and say, "Do you still think you are awake or are you already gone?"

The genius of this model is that by first asking if they think they are awake, he sends the subject's mind on a transderivational search to make sense of the question, causing a PGO spike. Then the next part of the comment, "...are you already gone?" is a double entendre. It could mean the subject is in hypnosis or that the subject has checked out of it. Either way, the subject must come to their own answer.

The double bind works very well in a one-on-one environment to get something you want. For example, say you like action movies and your spouse does not. Instead of asking, "What movie would you like to see tonight?" you position the question as, "Would you like to see the new James Bond movie or the new *Fast and Furious* movie tonight?" By giving your spouse two choices, they will likely forget that there are other choices. It is simply because whatever we bring focus to becomes the focus.

In advertising, we can use double binds to give the consumer two choices, both of them being the desired outcome we want. Following are some examples.

A candy company that asks which of their flavors is your

favorite and asks the question, "Will you choose grape or strawberry?" takes the viewer through the double bind. They presupposed that their candy is your favorite, drew your attention away from questioning that statement, focused your mind on the two flavors, and left you to think about which one you will buy rather than thinking about *if* you like it at all or would even buy it.

Think about a car company ad that states, "No matter if you choose the coupe or the convertible, you will love the way it makes you feel." The idea that you are in the market for a new car is presupposed; it is only a matter of whether you want the coupe or the convertible.

Recently, the restaurant chain Red Lobster employed a similar tactic. They ran a television commercial where they tell the viewer how excited they are that Lobsterfest is back. Before the viewer has time to think about whether a festival involving lobster is something that appeals to them, they are shown three different lobster dinners and asked which one they will choose.

Again, diverting your attention to the selection causes you to cease questioning if Lobsterfest is really everything that it is cracked up to be. So instead of deciding if you want to partake in Lobsterfest, you find yourself deciding which of the three dinners is the most appealing.

FEAR-BASED COMMUNICATIONS—YOUR LIZARD BRAIN IS IN CHARGE

Since the beginning of time, all people make decisions based on one of two criteria: avoidance of pain or seeking of pleasure. Often, people will challenge this model, but once they attempt to prove it wrong, they quickly convince themselves of its accuracy.

Of the two prime motivators, avoidance of pain is more powerful than the pursuit of pleasure. A person may first try cocaine or heroin for the pursuit of pleasure or the high, but eventually the addiction becomes driven by the avoidance of pain. The knowledge of the withdrawal symptoms and the idea of living life without the drug becomes an overwhelming pain to be avoided.

For most addicts, the only thing that drives them to a threshold of thinking and feeling that "there has to be change, it has to be now, and it has to be me," is when the pain of living the life of a drug addict exceeds the pain of withdrawal and not getting high.

Another example is the battered wife. Think about a woman living in an abusive relationship; it could be physical or mental. She knows she should leave him; her family and friends tell her to leave him, but she remains. The prime driver for her is her fear of the unknown. "How will I make it on my own?" "What will life be like without him?" "Will anyone else ever love me?" Only when the pain of being with the abuser outweighs the pain of not being with him will she make a change.

Why are humans so fear avoiding? To answer this, we turn to evolutionary psychology and the amygdala.

The amygdala is a small, almond-sized portion of the brain. It is accepted science that the amygdala is the oldest or most primal portion of the human brain, often referred to as the lizard brain.

The primary job of the amygdala is to keep us safe. This is the part of the brain that can tell the difference between a stick lying on the ground and a snake. It has primary authority over the rest of the brain as its job is keeping us alive.

The human body evolved over eons, slowly adjusting to life on the African savanna from which 98 percent of human ancestry has evolved. According to evolutionary psychology, the mind is shaped by the need to survive and reproduce, and so our emotions, communications skills, and language ability represent adaptations that enabled human ancestors to thrive.

Many of the human behaviors we exhibit today were tools we developed for self-preservation. As humans, we jealously guard our romantic partners, because competition for mates has always been harsh. As people, we cherish our family because it is in our evolutionary best interest to preserve our genes. Humans crave social interaction to encourage cooperation, which further increases our chances for survival. Many of these behaviors are innate; how we interact with one another is literally programmed into our DNA.

In the most recent research on the amygdala that was conducted at Besancon University Hospital (Bonnet et al., 2015), they set out to discover the role of the amygdala in human behavior using fMRI images (Functional Magnetic Resonance Images). Using fMRI machines, the researchers could watch which portions of the brain lit up or showed activity when the subjects were shown different images. When subjects were shown photos of dangerous situations, the part of the brain that lit up was the amygdala.

Neuroscience has spent years modeling the anatomical structures of the brain and identifying what portions are responsible for underlying emotions.

Science has explained how the amygdala processes information primarily visually, and then it transfers this information to other parts of the brain for reaction or storage.

A key bit of knowledge when marketing to this primal brain

is that the amygdala does not really discern whether an event is real or not. Imagine you are at the movies and you are watching a typical suspense/horror genre film. As the young, unsuspecting woman adventures down into the dungeon-looking basement, your heart begins to pound as you see the lunatic armed with a chainsaw hiding under the stairs.

As the young woman descends the stairs, ever so slowly, the tension and anxiety you feel continue to build, even causing you to think or say, "Look under the stairs!" Finally, the villain leaps out to attack the victim, and you suddenly jump or maybe even spill your popcorn, even though it is make-believe, and you knew what was coming.

The reason is simple. Your amygdala cannot tell that this is a fantasy on a movie screen. As far as your reptilian brain is concerned, you are in danger. Moviemakers know this and create films deliberately to take advantage of your reaction.

Another group that understands this reaction is the news media. The 24/7 news cycle survives on bad news. You rarely see anyone run a good news story, and certainly there is no "good news" channel. The reason for the lack of good news is that good news does not keep you alive, but a lack of bad news can kill you. Sadly, this nonstop flood of bad news coming at us from multiple devices is at the root of the epidemic levels of anxiety being experienced today.

Anxiety is now the number one psychological disorder in America. (*Anxiety and depression*, 1979).

Knowing that the amygdala is in charge and that it cannot tell the difference between reality and fantasy, we can leverage this into behavior for more effective marketing.

A great example of this was created by Volkswagen several years ago. In this television commercial, you see two people driving in a car. They are chatting and acting as two people in a car might typically behave. Suddenly, only a few seconds into the commercial, the car is violently hit directly on the driver's door and you as the viewer witness what it would be like to be in that car.

This sudden disruption triggers your amygdala and immediately makes you concerned about being broadsided in your own car. Then the spot transitions to the two occupants of the car being safe due to the superior airbag system available in the VW.

Although this is an extremely dramatic example, there are simpler and less disruptive ways we can use this. We can create the fear of aging if we do not take certain vitamins, the fear of being rejected if we have bad breath, or the fear of running out of money for retirement if we do not use a certain financial company.

VIII

BIASES

COGNITIVE BIASES—NO ONE IS NORMAL

Cognitive biases are defined by Wikipedia (Wikipedia, 2020) as "a systematic pattern of deviation from the norm or rationality in judgment, whereby inferences about people and situations may be drawn in an illogical fashion."

The theory or term *cognitive bias* was first intruded by Kahneman and Tversky in 1974 in their breakthrough article titled "Judgment under Uncertainty: Heuristics and Biases" (Kahneman & Tversky, 1974).

Cognitive biases describe irrational mistakes in human decision-making. Our brains take in a massive amount of information all day long. Some of the information we actually think about, but as our conscious brain has only limited capacity, we are really focused on one thing at a time. So, our brains are always looking for shortcuts.

It is important to understand cognitive biases. This understanding will lead to better use of language and imagery and will allow hypnotic and neuro-linguistic programming (NLP) to improve the outcomes of advertising.

There are many forms of cognitive biases, and some impact us on a regular basis. In particular: our children, religion, politics, our favorite sports team, and the unfairness of referees. However, for the sake of this book, we will primarily stick to the ones that matter most to the world of influencing and marketing.

AFFECT BIASES—SHOOTING FROM THE HIP

This is the effect of heuristics in judgment of risks and benefits. This type of bias allows people to make a quick and emotional response based on their gut feeling. Research shows that when a person has a pleasant feeling about something, they see the benefits as high and the risk as low and vice versa (Finucane et al., 2000).

As such, affect bias behaves as the first and fastest reaction in decision-making. It is the "shoot from the hip" response. The cause and effect does not necessarily have to be consciously observed. The speed can influence the judgment.

To measure this, participants were placed into a priming paradigm. They were shown a happy face, frowning face, or neutral face for 1/250 of one second. This is an amount of time where participants could not recall what they saw.

1/250 of 1 Second

Next, they were shown a Chinese character for two seconds and were asked to rate the character on a scale of liking. Research showed that the participants preferred the character that was preceded by the happy face over the frown or neutral face, even though it was shown only for 1/250 of a second.

This makes a strong argument for marketers to focus on the finite details of images, such as the settings and backgrounds that people see for even a split second. These images have the ability to prime the consumer to feel better about the product or service being presented. Some examples of this would include smiling people in the background, people having fun, and pleasant settings.

Affect Biases—Time: Cracking Under Pressure

Next, we turn our attention to include time. The above-referenced study (Finucane et al., 2000) looked at the affect biases created under time pressure. Researchers compared people under no time pressure versus those under time pressure. Their hypothesis was that people under time pressure would rely more on their affect or emotions rather than deep thinking or consideration.

To do this study, students were randomly assigned to one of two conditions (time pressure versus no time pressure) and one of two counterbalancing orders (risk judgment versus benefits judgment or vice versa). The students were then given a task in which they had to make judgments about the risk or benefit of certain activities and technologies.

As predicted, individuals in the time-pressure condition took less time to make risk judgments than did individuals in the no-time-pressure condition. The higher the benefit or the more the risk, the more impact time pressure had on their decision. Essentially, the bigger the bet, the more pressure that was felt from time.

Marketers have known for years the value of time-sensitive

offers and limited-supply claims. Finding credible ways to drive time pressure can create an environment for the consumer to spend less time thinking or considering an offer and thus act more quickly. However, credibility is key. As we know with hypnosis or NLP, nothing useful can take place without rapport. This also holds true in marketing.

To use this to our advantage, we want to lean into how our product or communications make people feel. As an example, a well-respected or beloved celebrity can have this effect, as the emotional response the person has for the celebrity can be passed on to the product or service even though there is no real connection between the two.

Affect Biases—Fear Appeals

Continuing with the affect biases is fear appeals. These are frequently used in health-related products or services as the marketers use fear to grab the consumer's attention. The way fear works is by creating an anxiety in the consumer's mind and convincing them the only solution to overcoming the fear is to buy and use the product being discussed.

In a study conducted in 2011 (Averbeck et al., 2011), researchers looked at how prior knowledge influences people's response to fear-based messaging.

Researchers found that when people had prior information

or knowledge of a subject, they exhibited less fear and were less prone to react to a fear-based message when compared to individuals who did not have as much information.

A good example of this is the "Dr. Google" syndrome. Many people type symptoms into websites like Google or WebMD in an effort to determine what they are experiencing. With little to no information or knowledge about a specific disease state, they see that their symptoms could be something totally benign or they could have cancer.

The reader immediately skips over the simple explanation and jumps to the deadly option, since without proper understanding of either condition, their mind goes to the most dreaded option—the one that generates the most fear.

The flip side of this phenomenon is also common. Patients with a greater understanding of their condition and practicing better mental health and visualization show a significantly higher and quicker rate of recovery (National Research Council, 2001).

For advertisers and marketers, this demonstrates great opportunity for companies making products that have health or medicinal claims. Leaning into the disease state using broad symptoms, while not getting too detailed, will work. This can be accomplished by demonstrating to the consumer that your product does address the problem currently being discussed. Keep in mind that in this case, less information is more. You want to leave the consumer feeling as if they have learned something new without making them work too hard to get the knowledge.

As an example, an advertiser may give a list of symptoms and then tell the viewer, "If you have three or more of these symptoms, you may be dealing with 'disease X.'" This allows the consumer to see themselves in the communication, but also lets them have an epiphany or the aha moment when they realize their symptoms are part of a condition that has a name.

A study done in 2008 (seven years removed from 9/11) found that people will pay more for flight insurance that is exclusively for terrorist attacks versus flight insurance that covers all causes (including terrorism). Why is that? It seems that the term "terrorist act" generated negative feelings and emotions, which in turn caused people to make an irrational choice: paying more for less coverage.

ANCHORING BIASES

This bias describes the human tendency to rely heavily on the first piece of information they receive. A great example of this is the old political ploy: "Senator, are you still beating your wife?" There is a tendency for people to lock on or anchor to the concept of the wife-beating while never asking the question of whether it ever actually happened. Since the question was the first piece of information that people heard, everything that came after it was a response to that comment and became secondary.

As previously cited under anchoring heuristics, one of the earliest experiments conducted by Kahneman and Tversky was to guess the age of death for Mahatma Gandhi (Kahneman, 2011). Part of the research group was asked if Gandhi died before or after the age of nine. The other half was asked if he died before or after the age of 140. After that, each group was asked to guess Gandhi's actual age at the time of his death.

These simple pre-suggestions influenced the participant's answers significantly. The participants who were asked if Gandhi died before or after the age of nine guessed he died at the age of 50. Those who were asked if he died before or after the age of 140 guessed that he passed at the age of 67.

Anchoring is a strong tool for price conditioning. Most people create a preconceived notion of the price and value of a product prior to shopping for it. In many cases the price that the consumer guessed at the time of consideration, prior to any actual shopping, was much lower than reality.

A personal example of this for me was several years back when my wife wanted to buy a baby grand piano for our home. I immediately estimated in my mind that this would be a $10,000 to $12,000 acquisition. Once we visited a piano store, I was immediately shocked to discover that they were priced at $25,000.

I became immediately anchored at the $25,000 price. When I was finally presented with an opportunity to buy the piano for $19,995, I was pleasantly surprised, even in light of the fact that I had previously only placed a value on it of $12,000.

If you are going to use anchoring, you must really know your demographic. Anchoring effects are weaker for people with higher cognitive abilities and those with experience buying the product you are selling. Think carefully how you structure your pricing and anchoring, or you can easily lose credibility.

From a communication standpoint, anchoring tells us as marketers that we want to be first with a claim and be out in front of any information that could be used to support us or defame us. An example of this would be packaging that says gluten-free when in reality every product in the category is gluten-free.

AVAILABILITY BIASES—KEEP SAYING IT UNTIL IT IS TRUE

Availability is the tendency of humans to default to the most recent or highly available information and consider it to be fact. As an example, if you were to ask most people which job is more dangerous: a police office or a logger, most people would choose the police officer.

Statistically, a logger is more likely to die on the job than a police officer. However, police deaths are highly publicized while logging deaths are not.

The importance for advertisers is first availability and second timing. The more available your message is, the more likely it is to be taken as fact. This is where frequency of messaging matters. The more people hear your message or "truth," the more they believe it.

The second issue for advertisers is timing or the term "recency." This means how close can you get your message to the consumer's point of need?

Imagine that you are sitting in the waiting room at your doctor's office. You are there to see him about what appears to be an allergy. While sitting in the office, you pick up a magazine to pass the time. As you are flipping the pages, you see an ad with the headline: "Finally real allergy relief." You are extremely interested in this story and immediately read on. The ad copy tells you about a new prescription medication that works on allergy symptoms just like yours.

Toward the end of the ad copy, you see the words, "Ask your doctor to prescribe X."

This new medication that you had previously never heard of now occupies your total attention, and you cannot wait to ask the doctor if you can try it.

BOUNDED RATIONALITY BIASES—TRUTH AND CONSEQUENCES

Herbert Simon first coined the phrase "Bounded Rationality" (Simon, 1957). Bounded rationality is derivative of utility theory, which refers to the usefulness or value that consumers experience from a product. The economic utilities help assess consumer purchase decisions and pinpoint the drivers behind those decisions.

Bounded rationality begins with the observation that humans like some consequences better than others, even if only hypothetically. A perfectly rational person is one whose comparative assessment of a set of consequences works to maximize expected utility. However, we now know that humans do not make decisions perfectly or even rationally.

We are all limited by the information that we have. It is impossible to know everything. This places a cognitive limitation on our mind due to time constraints. This leads us to make decisions that are satisficing, rather than optimal.

The importance this plays in marketing is that we can create communications in many cases that will address the minimum bar that a consumer desires and trigger a response. Bounded rationality and the utility theory also teach us that consumers do not make decisions based on the best rational choice (Kahneman & Tversky, 1986), but on a number of factors such as emotion, information availability, and even ego-driven factors.

CERTAINTY BIASES—THE SURE THING IS NOT ALWAYS A SURE THING

Certainty effect or biases is the psychological effect resulting from the reduction of probability to probable. This came out of prospect theory, which was a challenge to utility theory. The difference between them is that utility theory decision-makers who have a 50 percent chance of winning will weigh that as exactly a 50 percent chance of winning, whereas prospect theory decision-makers treat decisions as a function of decision weights, meaning that people will often make irrational choices based on their emotions and feelings, not on the laws of probability or outcomes.

Normally a reduction in the probability of winning a reward creates a mental effect such as displeasure to people, leading to the perception of loss from the original probability, thus favoring the risk-averse decision. But the same reduction results in a larger mental effect if it is done from certainty rather than from uncertainty.

Here is one of Kahneman's examples:

> Which of the following options do you prefer?
>
> A. A sure gain of $30
> B. An 80 percent chance to win $45 and a 20 percent chance to win nothing

In this case, 78 percent of participants chose option A, while 22 percent chose option B. This demonstrates the typical risk-aversion phenomenon in prospect theory and framing effect, because the expected value of option B ($45 × 80 percent = $36) exceeds that of A by 20 percent (Kahneman, 2011).

Now consider this problem:

> Which of the following options do you prefer?
>
> A. A 25 percent chance to win $30 and a 75 percent chance to win nothing
> B. A 20 percent chance to win $45 and an 80 percent chance to win nothing

In this case, 58 percent of participants chose B while 42

percent chose option A. As before, the expected value of the first option ($30 × 25 percent = $7.50) was 20 percent lower than that of option B ($45 × 20 percent = $9). However, when neither offer was certain, risk-taking increased.

The lesson for marketers is how to use language to craft an offer that gets the best response. An offer that says, "We are holding a sweepstakes and 100 people will win $1,000" would have a greater effect than saying, "We have one winner of $250,000" even though the amounts are dramatically different ($1,000 × 100 = $100,000) versus ($250,000 × 1= $250,000). The former offer increases the odds, is more certain, and therefore is interpreted to be the better offer.

COMMITMENT BIASES—WHY WE DOUBLE DOWN

Commitment bias is extremely powerful and difficult, if not impossible, to recognize in one's self. This is also known as the sunk cost fallacy. It was originally described by Barry Straw in his 1976 paper, "Knee deep in the big muddy: A study of escalating commitment to a chosen course of action" (Straw, 1976).

The bias is that people have a strong tendency to be congruent, meaning that we want to follow information, beliefs, and choices that are consistent with our self-image.

This bias explains why people stay committed to actions,

ideas, thoughts, and positions even when it is not in their own best interest. People rarely seek information that conflicts with their existing beliefs. Instead, we tend to interpret information as agreeing with us even when it does not. We seek data that reinforces our beliefs, and we ignore information that proves us wrong.

The importance of this is when we create marketing messaging. We need to be careful not to get so outside of a person's beliefs or self-image that they simply shut down and go into full disagreement with us. Even if we want to tell people information that disagrees with them, we need to start off framing the communication in a fashion that respects their current belief.

We can sometimes accomplish this with prequalifying statements. Or, in the language of Robert Cialdini, a presuasive statement.

Let us look at a communication experiment conducted by San Bolkan and Peter Andersen (Bolkan & Anderson, 2009). The purpose of this experiment was to show that social influencers can manipulate a person's self-image in such a way as to get the target to comply.

The study was run by having people carrying clipboards walk up to people in shopping centers and ask them if they would participate in a short survey. Following this approach, the researchers garnered a 29 percent compliance rate from the shoppers.

Using the same researchers and the same locations, the experimenters added a pre-question to the inquiry. Now as they walked up to the shoppers, clipboard in hand, they asked the would-be participant one question, "Do you consider yourself to be a helpful person?"

After a short time to think about this, nearly everyone said yes to that question. Then, right in the midst of this privileged moment, now that the shoppers had the time to proclaim both publicly and to themselves that they were a helpful person, the researchers asked, "Would you mind taking a short survey?"

As imagined, results or compliance went up, but what you may not have guessed is by how much. Compliance to take the survey now went to 77.3 percent. Remember, the result without the pre-question was 29 percent, so that is just shy of three times the results.

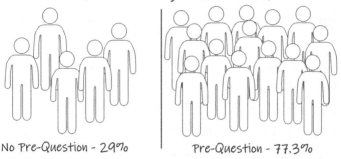

"Would you mind taking a short survey?"

No Pre-Question - 29%   Pre-Question - 77.3%

The reason for the massive jump in compliance is the commitment biases and the desire to be congruent. Once a participant publicly and privately proclaimed they were a helpful person, they had no choice but to prove they were helpful by taking the survey. Otherwise, they would have to live in an incongruent state, admit they were wrong, or change their belief system. Only 22 percent of people did that.

As a marketer, you must ask yourself, "What is our pre-qualifying question?" "What is the question I can ask that will force consumers to comply by leaning into their built-in desire to be consistent and congruent?"

If you were selling exotic vacations, you would first ask, "Do you have an adventurous spirit?"

If you wanted people to switch their brand of shampoo, you might try, "Are you always looking for the best products for your hair?"

No matter your question, it is important to position them in a fashion that is most likely to get an unqualified "Yes."

If your prime demographic is the parent of school-age children and the pre-qualifying question is, "Are you interested in your children's health?" it will be very difficult for a rational person to say no. Once they have said yes, they not only committed themselves to a specific position, but they also gave you permission to tell them how and what they can do for their children's health.

CONFIRMATION BIAS—YOU LIVE IN A BUBBLE AND SO DOES EVERYONE ELSE

This may well be the most important of all the biases. Confirmation bias reaches into many aspects of daily life and buying behavior. We will start with a broad overview, and then we will drill down into more specific areas.

Confirmation bias is the tendency to search for, interpret, favor, and recall information that confirms our already-held belief. It also explains why people interpret ambiguous, and sometimes conflicting, information as supporting their position. In other words, it is our internal "yes man."

As marketers, we have the opportunity to build and develop our customers' beliefs about our products and services. We have the chance to provide our consumers the evidence of the difference in our offering and help confirm their beliefs.

Why do consumers think brand names are better than store brands? Why do some people buy vitamins that do not work, but they keep taking them anyway?

One great example was from Rich Harshaw and how Holiday Inn Express turned the usually mundane issue of a showerhead into an advantage for their hotels. He never would have noticed the showerhead. He would have just taken for granted that the hotel shower had a showerhead.

But Holiday Inn ran advertising boasting about the new and unique showerheads they had. They asked what showerhead setting you would use when you visited their hotels.

> They tell you the showerhead is the greatest thing since sliced bread. Then when you actually get in the shower, you not only notice the showerhead, but you also interpret the evidence (large size, gourmet settings, high pressure) as proof that it is indeed great (Harshaw, 2014).

Just like the old Wisk campaign in the 1960s that essentially created "ring around the collar" as a problem that needed solving, Holiday Inn created a problem that travelers did not know they had by providing the payoff with the great showerhead; the consumer's own confirmation bias confirmed that indeed they did need this big showerhead.

Once our product has brand awareness, we can use confirmation bias to reinforce what the consumer thinks they already know about us. Amazon is associated with large selections and quick delivery. Even if Amazon does not have the product you want, or the product you ordered shows up a few days late, you do not change your opinion of Amazon. Your own confirmation bias tells you that this is just an anomaly and that Amazon is still fast. In other words, you will tell yourself you were still correct to order from Amazon.

Another example is Mac versus PC. Chances are you are either a Mac user or a PC user. Although PC users are rarely passionate about their computer, Mac users usually are. They will buy an Apple computer, iPad, and iPhone and have their entire connected life within the Apple universe.

Although I am a Mac user, I will admit that a PC computer with the same processing speed and capacity is about 30 percent of the cost of a comparable new Mac. The reality is, once people identify as a Mac user, they will use every available piece of information to justify this decision, such as a Mac's elegant design, speed, protection from viruses, lifetime use, etc.

More than being a user of a product, once a consumer associates themselves with a brand (think Harley-Davidson), it becomes part of their identity. Think of the people who are dedicated to wearing only Nike sportswear but are not athletes, or people who prefer to wear outdoor clothing from North Face yet have never participated in any outdoor sports.

Using confirmation bias, we have the opportunity to tell consumers what their problems are, and how we are the solution for them. However, our own confirmation bias can interfere with our creativity and development of great communications.

The marketer's job is to understand their target demographic, but our own confirmation bias can interfere with this. We then start to build an imaginary target based on who we think our consumer is. Many times, I have seen clients who are successfully selling a product to a 55+ demographic suddenly shift their advertising to a 25+ demographic for no other reason than they want their product to look young and cool. Even when we have presented overwhelming data showing who the target is, they still change the target.

A real-world example of cognitive bias killing a business was the restaurant chain Bill Knapp's. The chain of restaurants started in 1948 in Battle Creek, Michigan, and grew to 60 locations throughout Michigan, Ohio, Florida, and Indiana.

The original angle was family-style home-cooked food for multigenerational dinners. As time progressed, the multigenerational dinner model faded, but the restaurant held onto its senior citizen business and was successful in this demographic.

In 1998, the chain was sold to an entrepreneur from California. This new owner was convinced that he knew better, regardless of the fact that he bought the business because of its then-current success.

He introduced a campaign called *"That Was Then, This is WOW."* They did a complete revamp of the stores; hung shower curtains between tables; added video games, toys, graffiti on the walls, and loud color; and played loud rock and roll music.

Along with *"This is Wow"* décor changes, they revamped the menu, eliminated all the family foods that the seniors liked, and went to more trendy fare. They replaced homemade soups with Lipton mixes and homemade mac and cheese with Kraft powders to save costs.

The overhaul turned out to be a disaster for the chain. All of the changes drove the seniors away permanently, while none of the so-called "cool" changes attracted any young people. By 2001, Bill Knapp's did a complete about-face with a new campaign called *"Tradition is Back,"* but it was too late. The real demographic, which was seniors, had gone for good and established new restaurant habits. The chain filed for bankruptcy and closed its last location in 2002.

Confirmation bias also puts marketers at risk of wrongfully listening to the voice in our head or our internal "yes man." It can cause us to think that our idea for an ad campaign is the right one and to ignore market research or skip over A/B testing.

BIASED SEARCH—JUST TELL ME WHAT I WANT TO HEAR

Research has shown that people tend to search for information or evidence in a biased fashion. Rather than searching through all available information, we tend to focus on information that supports our current belief system. We tend to look for information that answers the question of, "What if I am right?" instead of looking for information that asks, "What if I am wrong?"

We tend to seek information that is delivered in a positive light (Baron, 2008). For example, using yes or no answers to find a number we suspect of being the number three, we might ask, "Is it an odd number?" People prefer this type of question, which is called a positive test, even when a negative test such as, "Is it an even number?" would yield the exact same answer.

The search for positive test is not in itself bias since it can produce good information, but when combined with other effects, it can lead to the confirmation of existing beliefs (Klayman & Ha, 1987).

In the real world, information is messy, mixed, and complex. As an example, we can come to different conclusions about someone based on what aspect of them we focus on. When we meet a new person, we make a very quick set of assumptions about them, which is called a "first impression." Every time we meet them in the future, we look for behaviors that confirm our first set of assumptions.

Even the way we phrase a question can alter the outcomes (Kunda, 1999). When people are asked the question, "Are you happy with your social life?" they report a much greater satisfaction with it versus when they are asked, "Are you unhappy with your social life?"

Even the slightest change in language can cause a significant change in outcome. This was demonstrated using a fictitious custody case (Shafir, 1993).

Participants read that parent A was moderately suitable to be the guardian in multiple ways. Parent B had a mix of positive and negative qualities: a close relationship with the child, but a job that would take them away for long periods of time. When asked which parent should have custody of the child, the majority of the participants chose parent B, looking for mainly positive attributes. However, when the question was changed to, "Which parent should not be given custody?" the participants went looking for negative information and again selected parent B.

Imagine how this could impact a marketing message. The simple process of asking consumers to find a reason to buy your product will have enormous implications as opposed to asking them why not to buy it. An example of a positive frame would be, "Out of all the features and benefits of our product, which one do you like best?" An example of a negative frame would be, "Knowing all the features and benefits of our product, what's preventing you from buying today?"

Intelligence, education, and confidence can have a major bearing on cognitive bias (Albarracin & Mitchell, 2004). An experiment examined the extent to which people could refute arguments that contradicted their personal beliefs.

People with high confidence levels more readily seek contradictory information to their personal position to form an argument. These heightened confidence levels decrease preference for information that supports an individual's personal beliefs. This is simply because the confidence a person has in their given belief results in more curiosity regarding the thoughts of others. Conversely, people with low confidence levels do not seek contradictory information and prefer information that supports their personal position. These people generate and evaluate evidence in arguments that are biased toward their own beliefs and opinions.

As a marketer, this is another important reason to understand your demographic. Are you talking to a highly educated and confident consumer, or are you talking to someone who lacks confidence?

When talking to a more confident consumer, you will be better positioned to challenge their current paradigm, while the less confident consumer will likely tune you out as soon as they detect a threat to their belief system.

DISCONFIRMATION BIAS—LIE TO ME, PLEASE

A subset of confirmation bias is a phenomenon called disconfirmation bias. This demonstrates that even when people are given the exact same information, individuals will interpret it differently.

A team of Stanford researchers conducted an experiment with people who had strong feelings either for or against capital punishment (Lord et al., 1979). Each person was given two fake studies to read. One study was pro-capital punishment and the other was anti-capital punishment.

Once the participants had read both of the studies, they were asked if either study influenced their position on the death penalty.

Participants who were pro-death penalty remained that way. The same was true of the anti-death penalty group. Participants from both groups claimed such things as the study "was not large enough" or "wasn't long enough," or that the researchers presented no clear case, all the while accepting the results of the survey that agreed with them. Keep in mind both presented studies were false.

The learning from this study is that people will readily accept studies or information that agrees with them while holding data that disagrees with them to a much higher standard.

The lesson for marketers is that if you can find statistical data that agrees with your consumers' present belief system, then you can use this as a means of providing credibility. If your facts run contrary to popular belief, make sure you are aiming at the more confident consumer. This is particularly true with political ads, where you will see one side quote a set of statistics and the other side use yet another set of statistics, while both sides are being technically correct.

CONFIRMATION BIASED MEMORY—YOU ARE REMEMBERING IT WRONG

People recall or remember information with an interpretation that best suits their beliefs. After all, we know that people strive to be congruent. This is referred to as selective recall or confirmatory memory.

There are two schools of thought on this. One model is that the mind recalls memories more easily when they agree with or confirm our belief system. The other model is that information that is more novel or surprising will have a higher recall value.

A selective memory test has also been conducted to show the desirability of personality types and that people desire to have these traits.

An experiment was conducted in which one group of participants were shown evidence that extroverted people are more successful than introverts, while a second group was told the complete opposite (Kunda, 1999).

After the participants read these studies, they were asked to participate in an unrelated survey. In the survey, they were asked to recall past situations where they had behaved in an introverted or extroverted fashion.

The people who read the stories showing introverts were

more successful recalled more memories of themselves as introverts, while the participants who read the story demonstrating extroverts were more successful recalled more extroverted memories of themselves.

The message for marketers here is that when we ask consumers a question, we need to make sure we posture it in such a way as to put the person in the right frame of mind. As an example, if we are selling a brand of wine, we may want to call out how it is socially popular and favored by people who enjoy hosting parties.

MYSIDE BIAS—DO NOT CONFUSE ME WITH THE FACTS

As we progress through the various types of confirmation bias, we next look at myside bias. This is how the accuracy of a memory is altered based on my belief structures.

A study was done using extra sensory perception (ESP) as its basis (Russel & Jones, 1980). A group of people were assembled with half claiming to believe in ESP and half claiming they did not. All participants were then shown studies with some supporting the existence of ESP and the other half not supporting it. In other words, they were presented with evidence to support both viewpoints. They were then asked to recall the information. Both groups recalled the information correctly except that the group of ESP believers recalled the information disproving ESP as actually proving it existed.

This demonstrated how people will alter their memory to support their belief system and basically only hear what they want to hear. Myside bias shows us that we can only take a consumer so far with alternate information before they start to rewrite our messages. It also is a warning to marketers that people will hear what they want to hear, so evaluate your message for clarity.

IRRATIONAL PRIMACY EFFECT—INFORMATION: WE WANT IT NOW

This is about people's preference for early information. Experiments have shown that information is weighted much more strongly when it appears first (or early) in a series of information, even if the order is unimportant. People form a more positive opinion of someone who is described as intelligent, industrious, impulsive, critical, stubborn, and envious than when they are given the exact same list of words in reverse order (Baron, 2008).

This is called an irrational primacy effect in which the earlier items in a series are recalled at a greater rate. What is at issue here is that people form a loosely defined hypothesis of the information they are receiving, so the first information forms the original thinking. The presentation order of the key points determined the importance of those key points. Think of it as the first part of the overall first impression.

An experiment was conducted using a slideshow of a single image. At first the image would be seen just as a blur, but subsequent showings extended the time on screen until it got to the point where it was clearly in focus (Barron, 2008). After each slide was presented, the participants had to guess what the image was. Participants who guessed wrong early in the experiment continued to guess wrong even when the image was clearly visible.

This offers two critical lessons for marketers. The first is the need for proper order. The most important or salient features or benefits of your product or service need to be called out up front. As noted earlier in this section, confirmation bias can color our own opinion of what is the most important feature of a product since we often base this choice either on what is most important to us or on a very unscientific model of listening to those around us. This is when using consumer surveys or panels can be helpful.

Let us assume you sell a diet product. Your product does many wonderful things for the consumer and you can list 10 different health benefits. Knowing people's tendency to irrational primacy, you need to order your communications with the most important feature first, then the second and third; then you must stop there. Because we know that our consumer's mind has limited capacity. (Remember, seven bits of information plus or minus two.) So, in the case of the diet product, it would be losing weight, burning fat, and feeling more energized. At this point it is not relevant that weight loss will help control diabetes, reduce joint pain, or help with neuropathy.

The second lesson we get from this reflects back to the slide experiment. If a person guesses wrong on what something is early on, they are likely to stick with the misinterpretation. We have all seen commercials like this: a couple is walking on the beach, perhaps with a dog, a sunset is in the background, and they are looking lovingly at each other. There are odd close-ups on body parts or smiles. This goes on for 25 seconds. Then in the last few seconds of the commercial we find out what the product is, and we see it is for some new herpes drug.

Now think of how the primacy effect is impacting the consumer. They may be wondering if it is a dating app. Maybe it is a toothpaste ad or a book on couples' therapy. Maybe it is about something for the dog. By the time the advertiser has revealed the reason they made the ad in the first place, the viewer is overwhelmed with possibilities, and as we know they are likely to stick with their first wrong guess regardless of the final product reveals.

Marketers must remember to "keep the main thing the main thing." Get to the point quickly, making sure, in an unambiguous way, that the consumer understands what we are talking about and that the prime feature, the thing that is in it for them, is clear, concise, and to the point.

SELF-ENHANCEMENT—I AM GOOD ENOUGH, I AM SMART ENOUGH, PEOPLE LIKE ME

Self-enhancement is the human drive to reinforce the existing self-image one has of themselves or the drive to seek positive reinforcement. Both of these phenomena are driven by confirmation bias (Swann et al., 1989). In this experiment, the researchers learned that a person who is given feedback that is incongruent with the person's self-image is less likely to remember the information than when the feedback positively reinforces their self-image. Participants reported that negative comments, or feedback that did not support their own self-image, was unreliable data, and more likely to be dismissed or forgotten.

This is where NLP and hypnotic language can really come into play in ad creative. Using language like, "You work hard," "Parents like you care," and the famous McDonald's line, "You deserve a break today," supports or boosts the recipient's self-image.

When we examine, "You deserve a break today," we see a four-word tagline that is literally perfect from a neuro-linguistic programming standpoint. Breaking down this message to the consumer, we start with "you." Not only is it primary in the message, but it addresses me personally. They are speaking directly to me.

Also primary is "deserve." This line is giving me recognition. It is telling me I have earned something from my hard efforts, or from the fact that I am a good person.

Next, we go to "break." By saying I deserve this break, McDonald's is giving me positive feedback that I work hard, and I have earned this recognition. You are supporting my self-image.

And finally, "today." This is a closing call to action, to do it now, today. Tomorrow will be too late; you have earned it right now.

A form of confirmation bias is at play when we think of frequency of impressions. As an example, think of the last time you bought a new car. Did it seem like there were a lot of them on the road? Let us assume you now buy a red pickup truck. You begin to notice, since buying this red truck, that everywhere you look, you see red pickup trucks, as if suddenly red pickup trucks just became popular.

What really happens in these situations is a form of confirmation bias. It is where your mind is now unconsciously searching for red pickup trucks in an attempt to prove your choice was correct. If everyone has one, you must be smart.

This comes into play with our marketing. Once we have gained the attention of a consumer, or better yet the desire, their unconscious mind will go searching for the proof of this being a good idea. Every message and contact we have with the consumer must be congruent, or it is a lost impression. This is why consistency of your brand is so critical. An interesting note is that, several months after writing this original manuscript, I bought a red pickup truck.

CULTURAL BIAS—SEEING THE WORLD YOUR WAY

Regardless of people's desire to see the world as one big homogenous melting pot, the reality is that people have different belief systems, cultural values, and mores based on ethnicity, religion, gender, sexual orientation, and political views.

This is why it is important to understand your demographic. Does your product specifically appeal to a certain group of people and, if so, why? Does it appeal based on the product fitting a certain lifestyle or behavior? Are you appealing based on cultural issues?

One example is the fashion line FUBU, which is an acronym for For Us, By Us. The line was started by Damon John, who at the time was a young entrepreneur who noticed that none of the fashion lines popular in the black community were actually owned or made by African American people.

John started his small line of product on a shoestring budget and began chasing up-and-coming hip-hop and rap artists in an attempt to get them to wear his clothing, thus giving his clothing line street credibility and cultural significance.

But what if the group you are marketing to is different than the actual people making the product? Can it be done with authenticity without appearing to be pandering to the audience?

Not paying attention to the details and nuances of your message can cost you dearly. Take Heineken, a German brand, premium beer. In 2018, Heineken ran a TV spot for their light beer. The 30-second ad showed a bartender sliding a beer past three people, all of whom were black, and the glass of beer landed in the hand of a light-skinned woman. The ad tagline said, "Lighter is Better."

This blew up on the beer brand. Popular rapper Chance turned to Twitter to call the brand out for being obviously racist and accused them of doing this deliberately to get free publicity. Others accused the German beer brand of being Nazis or white supremacists and using the ad as a secret dog whistle to tell white supremacists that Heineken is the beer for them.

Another example was from the retailer H&M. H&M is known for their fashion sense and being on top of culture, but by not having the right expert review, a particular ad turned bad fast for the retailer. In this case, H&M placed a photo on their website of two young boys wearing sweatshirts that the retailer had for sale in the children's department. One child was white, the other black.

The idea of demonstrating diversity was a solid choice. However, the white child was wearing a sweatshirt that said that he was a "Survivor of the Jungle," which seems simple enough. But the black child was wearing a sweatshirt that said he was the "Coolest Monkey in the Jungle."

People were outraged, accusing H&M of being blatantly racist. A simple switch of which child wore which sweatshirt could have prevented this mess from ever happening.

Not all advertising cultural mistakes are race-based. Gender issues are just as prominent. When Peloton released their Christmas ad showing a man buying his wife an exercise bike to get her in shape, there was an outcry from some women who felt the ad was sexist. Similarly, Mr. Clean ran an ad that said, "This Mother's Day get back to the job that really matters." The visuals of the ad showed a mother with her young daughter scrubbing a surface with a Mr. Clean Magic Eraser. Women throughout the country took this ad to mean that the most important thing that women can do is housekeeping.

There are also examples of brands that took calculated risks on being offensive and won. A perfect example of this is

Nike and the use of Colin Kaepernick, an ex-NFL player. Nike bet that even though they would run the risk of offending conservative voters who were against Kaepernick's habit of kneeling during the national anthem prior to NFL games, they would more than make up for it in increased loyalty from black and liberal consumers. Nike was correct, and sales surged after the Kaepernick commercial was released. As of late, the cultural shift has moved toward embracing such movements. The Black Lives Matter movement has helped turn Kaepernick, and subsequently Nike, into heroes.

When speaking about the decision to use Kaepernick, Nike founder Phil Knight said, "It was divisive because it jumped on America's biggest fault lines—race, patriotism, sports, and business." But according to Knight, that was kind of the point. "It doesn't matter how many people hate your brand as long as enough people love it," Knight told *Fast Company* last year (Beer, 2019).

One of the best examples of using cultural reference properly from a company that was not of the same demographic was a campaign I did years back for Queenella Chitlins.

First some background: Chitlins are a food that is historically served at holidays and are most typically consumed by Southerners and African Americans. Chitlins are pig intestines and are typically sold in a bucket unwashed. The process of cooking them can take all day as they must be washed, boiled clean, washed again, and then cooked. It is a difficult and highly unpleasant experience.

In this case, our client was not in the chitlin business; they were a machine manufacturing company that invented a system that would take chitlins, strip them, flush them out, and clean them in a single process. They then packed them in a clear bag, ready to cook and eat.

Our job was to talk to this demographic in a culturally sincere fashion and inform people of an entirely new process or way of preparing a food that they had established behaviors for, doing it their way for decades. This was a big task given that the client was not black, and we needed to change people's opinion about the product.

Through a mutual friend, I reached out to the TV actress LaWanda Paige. LaWanda played the part of Aunt Esther in the 1970s sitcom *Sanford and Son*, which starred Redd Foxx as Fred Sanford. LaWanda's Aunt Esther character was famous for yelling at Foxx's Fred, "God's gonna get you, Sucka!"

I called LaWanda and said I needed her help. I told her about the product and the challenges I had presenting this to the black community correctly. As we spoke, she said to me, "Oh honey, I grew up in East St. Louis on a pig farm. My momma always made me clean the chitlins. Oh honey, it was awful!" LaWanda proceeded to write the entire TV commercial. LaWanda's own real story became the opening line of the TV commercial, followed with, "But with Queenella super clean chitlins, it's just open, cook, and eat."

Wanting to lean back into what was a cultural universal truth, which was that chitlins traditionally came in a bucket, and tying it into the phrase that made LaWanda famous, which was yelling the word "Sucka," we ended the spot with LaWanda saying, "So kick the bucket, Sucka!" and the embedded command to the viewer to "get Queenella super clean chitlins now at your local grocery store."

This ad hit right before Thanksgiving, a traditional time to serve chitlins. The success of the ad was so overwhelming that grocery retailers stopped putting them in the cooler and just rolled pallets of the product on the floor. It became the number one selling SKU to pass through the register scanner that year in all major grocery stores located in predominantly black communities.

This ad worked because we leveraged the good feelings and memories people had for LaWanda Paige. The ad was authentic because it was not some made-up story, it was her story. It also had a universal truth in it, had a cultural anchor (Sucka), and had an embedded call to action. Remember, when working in this space, people will sniff out a phony every time. Your messaging must be authentic.

BANDWAGON EFFECT OR SOCIAL PROOF BIAS

This is a cognitive bias that can be vital for the promotion of consumer-packaged goods as well as political campaigns and organizations. The premise is that people are more likely to buy a product or vote for a candidate that everyone else is.

The term social proof was first coined by Robert Cialdini in his 1984 book *Influence* (Cialdini, 1984). Social proof is prevalent in situations when people are not sure what to do, what brand to buy, or whom to vote for. We make an unconscious assumption that the larger group is smarter than we are individually, that the more people follow a certain pattern, the more likely it is to be the correct one.

Uncertainty is at the core of social proof. The more we see ourselves as similar to others around us, the more likely we are to adapt to the behavior of those around us. This is highlighted in the popular phrase, "When in **Rome, do** as the Romans **do**," which is frequently simply shortened to "When in Rome."

Another example of social proof or bandwagon effect is seen in TV sitcoms. The purpose behind laugh tracks in sitcoms is that people will laugh longer and harder with the inclusion of a laugh track because others, even canned voices, are also laughing. We think we are missing the joke if we do not laugh at the same rate as those around us (Platow et al., 2005).

A study on social influence was conducted using the premise of eyewitness identification (Baron et al., 1996). Subjects were shown a picture of a suspected criminal. They were then shown a lineup photo with four people, one of which was the suspect, and were asked to pick him out of the lineup.

The process was made more difficult by showing them the first photo very quickly, which is similar to how an eyewitness account might happen. The participants were four witnesses, but only one of them was a real participant; the other three were plants to help with the experiment.

The actors deliberately gave the wrong answer, influencing the real participant to agree with them 51 percent of the time. The reason is we often believe the group is smarter than we are.

As marketers, social influence can work both for us and against us. Let us address the latter first. There are three main ways for social influence to work against us.

First are bad online reviews. People now place a high level of importance on reviews. Amazon now outranks Google for people reading reviews, even when they intend to buy the product in a brick-and-mortar store. Travelers will often not book a hotel or a resort without first reading the reviews of visitors. Because of this, it is critical that every marketer has a proactive social media presence and review program in place.

The second place it can hurt a marketer is in focus groups. A typical focus group consists of six to ten participants, plus a moderator. The goal of a good moderator is to ask very specific, neutral questions that will not influence the outcome of the group. Typically, there is a two-way mirror where the marketing people sit in order to observe the responses without impacting the answers.

What happens is the focus group turns into a jury room. As with any group of people, there are always going to be one or two stronger Type-A personalities with the balance being more passive follower Type-B people.

The stronger personalities in the room will be the first to comment on the product being reviewed, expressing their "expert" opinion on why it is or is not a good product. They will share how they have had similar experiences or why they are an expert. One by one, the Type-B people will start to lean or even acquiesce to the stronger personality in the room. The result is you get the opinion of one to two people repeated five times.

While on the subject of focus groups, there is another social phenomenon that must be considered. It is the Hawthorne Effect, also known as the observer effect. The term was coined in 1958 by Henry Landsberger (Corporate Finance Institute, 2020) while doing research at the Hawthorne Works plant, a Western Electric plant outside of Chicago.

The outcome of the research was that the behavior of workers changed by the mere fact that they were being observed. They discovered that if the workers were aware that they were being observed as part of the study, their behavior changed. But when the observation was done, the behavior returned to the previous baseline.

Now let us put this to work in the focus group. You have recruited six consumers from the public at large, probably filtered through some type of demographic profile for age, gender, children at home, etc. You now place these people in a room full of strangers with an all-mirrored wall and you expect them to act like a natural consumer.

The fact that they are being observed, combined with the bandwagon effect, makes observing any real behavior impossible. This marketing amateur now feels they are expected to be a marketing expert. No one wants to appear incompetent, and yet the participants have no idea what is expected of them. So, they look for cues from the more powerful people in the room and find reasons to try to sound smart by agreeing with them.

What you end up getting from the focus group is one or two opinions and the remaining people trying to tell you not what they actually think, but what they think makes them look insightful.

The last way that social proof or bandwagon effect works against us is when it is working well for our competition. When our competitors are basking in the light of thousands of five-star reviews on Amazon or hundreds of social media influencers are talking about their product, it can be tough to overcome that. To do this, we first must identify a problem that the consumer believes and lead them to believe that the five-star product cannot address it. By doing this, we negate the impact of their reviews since none of them will be based on this new consumer need.

Now let us look at how social proof can help us. For products and services, the frontline effort needs to be in positive reviews. Marketers need a proactive approach to curating as many positive reviews as possible. You should include reviews in your communications. Show your product's five-star reviews on banner ads and websites. Incorporate the reviews into the ad copy. Use real customer testimonials when possible. Focus on past success. People want to buy what everyone else is buying because consciously (or unconsciously), we want to fit in and do not want to be left out. Unconsciously, the individual believes that the group's intelligence exceeds their own. This can be seen in various game shows over the years, such as *1 vs. 100* or when the contestant on *Who Wants to Be a Millionaire* would poll the audience to get help answering a question. (Interestingly, the audience was usually right!)

Social proof bias is the reason McDonald's demonstrated their mastery of neuro-linguistic programming for years with their use of outdoor signs telling people how many billions of hamburgers they had already sold.

What is the language that you can use? Phrases such as "Trusted by over one million moms," "Number one pharmacist recommended" and 'The official brand of NASCAR." These are just examples, but every brand has their unique story that can drive social proof.

SALIENCE BIAS—DO NOT BORE ME WITH THE DETAILS

Salience Bias, also known as perceptual salience, is a form

of cognitive bias that predisposes people to focus on items that are most relevant, prominent, or emotionally stimulating while ignoring those that are mundane or unremarkable, even when the true difference is irrelevant.

An example would be COVID-19. Individuals who know someone firsthand who has contracted the disease are far more likely to report that they think they could get it as compared to people who have only experienced it through the news media.

Other examples would be a red dot mixed amongst a sea of blue dots, or a loud noise in a quiet room. It is anything that stands out from the norm or is in contrast to its neighbors.

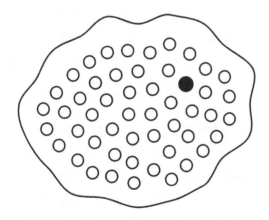

When the attention is driven by external stimuli, it is called Bottom Up/Memory Free, such as the loud noise in the quiet room. Conversely, attention can also happen from the

Top Down/Memory Dependent. Say you are going to cross the street. You perform a top-down search looking for the anomalies based on previous memory. Regardless, humans have great difficulty focusing on more than one thing at a time, so our unconscious minds are constantly having to prioritize different bottom-up and top-down influences.

A part of the brain known as the hippocampus helps with assessing salience by drawing on past memories and using them to filter new incoming data. It then takes the most important memories and places them into long-term memory.

What this means for marketers is that consumers tend to buy products that stand out from the others, as long as the category of product has not been commoditized in the consumer's mind. Marketers can leverage this bias by making unique and attention-gaining packaging or labeling that stands out in the mind of the consumer.

In addition to packaging, calling out unique features really matters in order to stand out from the sea of sameness. The use of certain trigger words or phrases will help reinforce salience, such as "exclusive," "patented," or "only available in..." Think about how "Intel Inside" and their familiar ring tone immediately pulls your attention to the fact that a device has an Intel chip in it, which drives a message in consumers' minds that it must mean the device is better than a competitor's.

EXPOSURE EFFECT—SEEING IS BELIEVING

This bias is based on the exposure or visibility of a product. An example is when products are placed on an endcap at retail. Major retailers actually charge marketers large sums of money to put their product on an endcap shelf as opposed to the regular, in-aisle shelf. Even when the product on the endcap is two feet away from the aisle where the product typically sits on the shelf, the endcap can produce as much as 10 times more in sales. This is simply from exposure bias. If the store makes the product more prominent, the consumer unconsciously raises the importance of the product. The more important the consumer feels a product is, the more valuable and desirable the product. Therefore, in-store positioning and promotion should be considered as part of an advertising strategy.

GROUP OR TRIBAL BIAS—MY GROUP CAN BEAT YOUR GROUP

Sometimes referred to as in-group favoritism or In-Group/Out-Group Bias is a pattern of favoring members of one's own in-group over that of the out-group. Studies have shown that in-group favoritism can result in the formation of cultural groups. Some examples would include music genre fans, Comic-Con attendees, sports affiliations, religious affiliations, and the like. These different groups can be separated by what on the surface would seem like trivial differences (Efferson et al., 2008).

Robert Cialdini and his research team studied the habits of university students wearing team T-shirts. The study showed that on the day after a win, the number of people wearing a team T-shirt increased significantly (Cialdini et al., 1976).

What was learned from this study is that people tend toward their own tribe and that personal identity is often derived from their tribal membership. In advertising, our communications reflect the language, style, clothing, ethnicity, and behaviors of the group we are targeting.

There is a chemical basis for some of this behavior. Research conducted by Carsten de Dreu shows that oxytocin enables trust and good feelings toward a person in group therapy. Oxytocin is sometimes called the "love neurotransmitter." It is the chemical the brain releases in response to love and affection. This spike of oxytocin can explain why people display strong favoritism toward their own group, family, and friends (De Dreu, 2012).

Realizing the value of in-group favoritism or tribalism, we can design our communications to launch this oxytocin hit every time a consumer encounters our brand. This can literally help consumers fall in love with your brand or product. For examples of this in action, watch the reaction of a child that identifies with Mickey Mouse when they walk into Disneyland, or visit a Harley-Davidson store and see how many Harley fans visit the store just to hang out and shop what might be new. It is because they do actually "love" the brand.

Marketers can lean into tribalism in several ways. We can use talent or images that best reflect the people or tribe that we are trying to market to, since people will most trust people who remind them of themselves.

We can also push into group tribes with sports sponsorships, athletes as spokespeople, or colleges. Additionally, we can lean into one's religious background, education, income levels, personal passions, or even causes.

As marketers, when we are making media choices, we can design our media plan around the tribes. On television, we would focus on Fox News to reach republicans or CNN for democrats. We can buy commercials on car shows to reach car enthusiasts, cooking channels for chefs, or HGTV for home improvement fans. The same holds true for satellite radio as there are hundreds of niche channels. And of course, magazines tend to be all about specific interests and lifestyles.

When we target specific media outlets, it is often necessary to customize or alter the creative to fit the group. An example would be delivering the same message using a famous conservative spokesperson on Fox News, while utilizing a well-known actor on CNN.

Another popular technique that leverages both tribalism and social proof is to run social media campaigns based on the platform's "Likes" feature. An example would be if you are looking at Facebook and you see an advertisement, but on top of the ad it says that a good friend of yours liked it. Not only has a member of your tribe endorsed this, but you now have the social proof to back it up.

ZERO RISK BIAS—I GUARANTEE IT

The job of any good advertising effort is to not only inform the public of a great product or service that may enhance their lives, but to help consumers overcome their own fears. Consumers fear making a bad decision, being ripped off, or looking foolish for buying something for which others may ridicule them.

As we discussed earlier in this book, people make decisions based on the pursuit of pleasure or the avoidance of pain. Of these two motivators, avoidance of pain is the stronger motive. Whenever a consumer is considering a new product, they internally weigh the pleasure versus the pain. They unconsciously ask themselves, "Does the risk of buying this outweigh the potential gain?"

If the risk-reward ratio is in equilibrium or 50/50, the consumer will likely not buy the product since the increased risk or fear will tip the scales. As marketers, to tip them back in our favor, we must mitigate the risk. This is best done through the use of guarantees.

Years ago, a client came to us with a very unremarkable over-the-counter product. The product was significantly overpriced for the category and did not offer any major technological advantages compared to other products it competed with. At the time we met the client, the product was not selling; it was failing and about to be removed from the shelf by major retailers.

So, we created the *Empty Container Guarantee*. The way the guarantee worked was the consumer could buy the product, take it home, use every last drop of product, and send the empty container back for a full, no-questions-asked refund. In the mind of the consumer, we just took the riskiest choice in the store, the highest priced product, and made it the lowest risk brand on the shelf.

But there was a secondary effect from this. When the marketer took this bold action and made it the centerpiece of their advertising, it changed the public's perception of the product. Consumers started to think that "any company willing to give me a full refund after I have used up the entire product must be very confident in the quality of the product." This not only lifted sales, but it lifted customer expectations. This display of confidence and near bravado gave the consumer more confidence in the product. The consumer went into the experience with the mindset that a product this expensive and with this guarantee must be good.

With the new, bold creative and a strong brand promise, that product that was failing at retail became the number one product in their category in all drugstores nationwide.

IX

INFLUENCING OR PERSUADING BELOW THE SURFACE

As discussed earlier in the grape and the beach ball analogy, the seven bits of information means that by using NLP we can reach past the conscious mind to the unconscious mind and help make immediate changes in behavior and belief systems. Imagine this as an iceberg. There is some small portion up top, but just as the bulk of the iceberg is underwater, the bulk of the communication happens under the surface. We can use NLP to create major improvements in our communication. Again, like hypnotherapists, we can reach past the conscious mind to the unconscious mind and help make immediate changes in behavior and belief systems.

CHOICE OVERLOAD—MORE DOES NOT MEAN BETTER

We often assume that more selection leads to more sales or even more customer satisfaction. However, this is not always true and more often than not, larger selection works against us in sales. This is called the paradox of choice. When a person is presented with too many options or choices, they become less likely to buy.

In 2000, psychologists Sheena Iyengar and Mark Lepper from Columbia and Stanford published a study now referred to as the Jam Experiment (Iyengar & Lepper, 2000).

On a regular day at a local food store, consumers were shown a display table with 24 different kinds of jam. Then on another day in the same store and on the same table, the selection was reduced to only six jams.

The researchers discovered that while the 24 types of jam table generated more interest, people were far less likely to buy a jar of jam by a factor of 10 compared to the same table displaying only six jams. While choice seems appealing, choice overload can cost us actual business.

Sales volume was not the only causality of the greater choices. The researchers also found that out of the people who did buy jam, those who bought it from the 24-choice table were less satisfied with the purchase than the people who only knew about the six choices.

Since the original study in 2000, there has been continued research in this area and it produces the same result. In an extensive study (Chernev, 2015), researchers analyzed 99 different choice studies and specifically looked for cases when increasing choices increased sales. Out of the 99 studies that were done, they never discovered any information that contradicted their original findings.

The researchers found four criteria that motivated consumers to buy. It is when:

1. People want to make a quick and easy purchase.
2. The product is complex (fewer choices help a consumer make a decision).
3. It is difficult to compare alternatives.
4. Consumers do not have a clear preference.

Once again, less is more.

DECOY EFFECT—BAIT AND SWITCH

This is when people who typically had two options were presented with a third, often decoy, option. The example is if a movie theater offers a $5 bucket of popcorn and a $10 bucket of popcorn, most people will choose the $5 bucket. Now insert a size in the middle and make it $8.50 and most people will go for the $8.50. The decoy was the $10 bucket that was used to price condition the consumer.

The reason is the $5 bucket looks like a value compared to the $10, but when the $8.50 option comes in, then the middle option has the appearance of being the best value. Keep in mind, no one buys the lowest price; they buy the highest perceived value.

This is important for marketers when it comes to price strategy and how to best position yourself within your category of business.

DUNNING-KRUGER EFFECT—TOO STUPID TO KNOW YOU ARE STUPID

Dunning Kruger Effect is cognitive bias in which people of low ability or skill overestimate their intelligence or ability. The original study was conducted by Dunning and Kruger in 1999 (Dunning & Kruger, 1999).

The study was first triggered by the researchers observing the case of McArthur Wheeler, a bank robber who was convinced that covering his face in lemon juice made him invisible to surveillance cameras because a friend told him this, and he believed it to be true. Even after being properly identified and arrested, he stood firm in his belief that the police could not have identified him from the cameras. To add to his stupidity, he told the police they could not see him because he was covered in lemon juice. (However, he did smell lemony fresh!)

Dunning wrote that people with substantial, measurable deficits in their knowledge or expertise lack the ability to recognize those deficits and, therefore, despite potentially making error after error, tend to think they are performing competently when they are not. In short, those who are incompetent, for lack of a better term, have little insight into their incompetence. Poor performers are in no position to realize they are poor performers.

Why is this important? First, it demonstrates the wisdom in the old saying, "Never get in an argument with an idiot. He will drag you down to his level and beat you with experience." But more importantly, it tells you to not try to change the mind of someone who is wrongfully stuck in their ways. Instead, find a way to lean into and reframe your message to fit their framework of truth. We need to meet the consumer where they are, not where we are. It is not the job of a company making a sugary dessert product to notify consumers of the dangers of diabetes, nor is it the responsibility of a credit card company to tell you how you should manage your money.

So, if you are selling mortgage refinancing to people who have mismanaged their money, as marketers we will tell them what they want to hear. They deserve the loan, and it is okay to use it to go on vacation, or buy new furniture. Let us say you have a weight loss product. Is it really in your best interest to tell people that they have gained too much weight due to overeating, lack of willpower, and not exercising? Or will you be better off to tell them that maybe their excess weight was the fault of not taking your product? Marketers are better off and more effective when they present the consumer with the simplest solution. Indeed, Occam's Razor postulates that the simplest solution is most often the right one.

REVERSE DUNNING-KRUGER—YOU WOULD HAVE TO BE REALLY SMART TO BE THAT CLUELESS

I am discussing this not so much for the benefit of creating good ad copy, but as a warning about the risk of bad copy.

The theory behind Reverse Dunning-Kruger effect is that individuals with exceptional knowledge or skill in a specific area are prone to overestimate the intelligence of those around them. Just like under-skilled people overestimate their real capabilities, highly skilled people tend to underestimate their highly refined skills.

Think of a time when an expert, say a doctor, started to explain something using terms and acronyms that you have never heard before. It is less likely that the expert was showing off or talking down to you, and more likely they just assumed that everyone knew what they did since it seemed simple to them.

As marketers, you run this risk. You know your product or service better than anyone else. Marketers tend to want to share every detail and feature of a product and want to share the benefits that most excite them. We need to keep our focus on our consumer and what is the most important thing about our product in their mind, not ours. We need to assume they know little to nothing about our product (unless we are speaking to experts) and talk to them from a very simple and fundamental basis. Never assume the consumer has our knowledge or even passion.

TIME DISCOUNT/PRESENT BIAS—CALL NOW!

This is also known as hyperbolic discounting. People have a tendency toward getting a reward now versus one in the future. People tend to value something in the future as lower value versus present day.

The most important thing about hyperbolic discounting is that it creates temporary preferences for small rewards that occur sooner over larger, later ones. People displaying hyperbolic discounting reveal a strong tendency to make choices that are inconsistent over time. They make choices for today that their future self would prefer not to have made, despite knowing the same information. This happens because hyperbola distorts that relative value of the options with a fixed difference in delays in proportion to how far the choice maker is from the options.

Payday loan stores and rent-to-own centers live off this thinking. A rent-to-own center will advertise a $400 flat screen TV for only $28 per week, making it within reach for many people who do not have the $400. However, the purchaser will end up paying $1,500 for that $400 TV over the life of the contract. The consumer will look back on the decision in the future and regret it, but the more hyperbolic the behavior, the more likely they will do it again.

Politicians and government agencies have long argued that the reason these people buy into these marketing models is a lack of education. Their solution has been to make the agreements easier to understand and include warnings in the contracts before people sign them, with the belief that it is just a lack of information and experience issue. However, all these changes have had little effect on these businesses.

THE NOVELTY FACTOR—WHY LIFE SPEEDS UP OVER TIME

Think for a moment about a place you enjoy and have been to several times. It may be a cabin in the woods, a vacation rental in a warm climate, or even a favorite hunting or fishing spot.

Now think about the first time you were there and recall all the details. You will find that you can recall many things about it, how it looked, how it felt, how it smelled, lights, colors, all the details that went into this experience for the first time.

Now recall the third or fourth time you have been there. Chances are you cannot. If you are like most people, the most vivid memories you have of this place are only the first and the last. You remember the first time because of novelty. It was new. It was an experience you never had before. Your brain had to create new memories that never existed.

The reason you remember the last visit is due to recency, or how your brain records the most recent events. (An exception to making the first and last memories stand out might be if, as an example, the third time you went was the first time you took your family to the location. In this case, you will have created new memories as you had a first-time experience of seeing the location through the eyes of another person who is important to you. You reexperience it through people you care about.)

The bottom line is that memory is created out of novelty, and novelty is how we experience time. As an example, one day in the life of an 11-year-old child would be expressed as the fraction 1/4,000, but one day in the life of a 55-year-old would be expressed as 1/20,000. As you can see, for the 11-year-old a single day represents 2½ times more time when compared to their entire life.

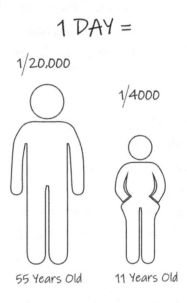

1 DAY =

1/20,000

1/4000

55 Years Old   11 Years Old

What it demonstrates to us is that the older the person is that we are marketing to, the more value salience or novelty will have to them because they are more likely to have already experienced something similar. In short, the older the target demo, the greater the need for novelty.

Einstein was asked to explain relativity or time. He explained it like this: Imagine you are standing in front of a hot stove. Someone takes your hand and holds it against the stove for 10 minutes. Next, imagine you are deeply in love. The person you are in love with must go away for two years, and you only have 10 minutes with them before they leave. As we can see, 10 minutes is not always experienced in the same way. The 10 minutes at the stove will feel like an eternity, but the 10 minutes with your love will feel like seconds. How we experience time is greatly dependent on the life event.

The model is important to us as marketers since we have the ability to create novelty in the consumer's life. We can create situations or messages that are unique, never before experienced, brand-new thoughts. These novel experiences will cement in the memory at a far greater rate than information to which the consumer has previously been exposed. This novelty gives us the advantage of being remembered for a longer period of time, which will result in better recognition at the moment of purchase.

TAGGING, YOU ARE IT!

This is a simple advertising copywriting technique designed to force the consumer into agreeing with your comment. In other words, you are hijacking the consumer's thinking process by quickly pushing them into agreement with you. The more consumers agree with us, the more likely they are to become a customer.

Tagging is done by adding anywhere from one to three words to the end of a sentence or a thought, making the comment a universal truth. Examples of words and phrases to add are "Right?" "Isn't it?" "Can't you?" "Don't you?" "Aren't they?" "Is it not?" and "Did you not?".

Note the difference between the statement, "Saving money feels good" and the tagged statement, "Saving money feels good, right?" One tells a consumer something they need to think about. But the tagged message presupposes the answer and prompts the consumer to agree.

"Saving money feels good, right?" "You want to feel younger, don't you?" "Bad breath is so embarrassing, don't you agree?" "No one should have to wake up in the middle of the night with leg cramps, isn't that right?" and "When you are feeling sick, you want something that works fast, don't you?"

The idea is to make a bold, definitive statement as if it is a universal truth, then tag it in a very closed-ended statement that would require the person hearing it to agree with it. No one can honestly say that they would not want a fast-acting treatment when they are sick, or that waking up with leg cramps is a good thing. By closing the loop, you moved the statement from being your truth to being their truth.

WHEN X THEN Y—WE ARE NOT TALKING CHROMOSOMES

As discussed earlier, the human mind is a pattern-recognition machine. Our minds search for patterns, identify with patterns, and operate on patterns. When we walk into the shower in the morning, we do not stare at the faucet trying to figure out how it works; we have already developed a pattern for making it work. When you get in your car, you do not have to think about how it starts, how you make it move forward, and how to turn it. You have already developed a pattern. This pattern is so well refined that you can drive to work in the morning on autopilot and never even pay attention to how you got there.

Knowing that people are pattern-recognition machines allows us to pattern language that will play into this. This is where we use the words "when" and "then." By using language that the mind recognizes, the pattern will allow the comments to become consumers' truths.

"When" allows us to reframe the past: to establish an event in the consumer's mind regardless of if it really happened or not. "Then" lets us pre-frame or presuppose their future.

An example would be, "When you drive a Cadillac, you will be the envy of your neighborhood."

The phrase, "When you drive a Cadillac" reframes the past.

We do not say, "IF you drive a Cadillac." We say, "WHEN you drive a Cadillac," as if it has already happened.

Now look at the second half of the sentence: "you will be the envy of your neighborhood." Notice we did not say, "You MAY be the envy." We are telling them, "You WILL be the envy." Again, we are presupposing that this is a given, that it is a foregone conclusion.

One last thought on this is the use of the phrase: "You don't have to." You can add a comment at the end of an XY statement as a way of lowering the person's internal stress level. It relaxes them to think and feel that no one is demanding them to do anything.

Regardless of adding "You don't have to," the technique still works because the unconscious mind, which is what rules most buying decisions, is literal in nature.

THE LITERAL UNCONSCIOUS AND EMBEDDED COMMANDS

Under Freud's psychoanalytical model of human personalities, the unconscious mind is a reservoir of feelings, thoughts, and urges that lie deep below the surface much like the way an iceberg is mostly below the waterline and hidden from sight.

We have learned through hypnosis that the unconscious

mind is very literal in nature. As any of us who practices hypnotherapy has witnessed, when we have a subject in a deep hypnotic trance, we always get a literal answer to any question we ask. As an example, if I were to ask you, "Do you know your name?" you will probably respond by saying your name. That is because it is your conscious mind that provides you with the interpretation of what was meant by the question.

But if we ask the same question under hypnosis, you will likely respond with the one-word answer, "Yes." This is because, in a literal fashion, "Do you know your name?" is a yes or no answer. In the hypnotic state, the unconscious mind provides the literal answer.

Knowing the literal nature of the human mind allows us to create such things as embedded commands. This is a technique used in hypnotherapy but can also be used in ad copy. As an example, we give a direct message of "Go to CVS now and buy X." We pre-frame the command with a softer comment and then post-frame it with other copy. The direct order goes unnoticed by the conscious mind but goes directly, literally into the unconscious mind.

SPEAKING VISUALLY AND AVOIDING ABSTRACTS

Have you ever noticed that if you have a child eating food in a high chair and you instruct the child, "Do not throw food on the floor," that he nearly immediately throws the food on the floor? It is not because the child is being rebellious; it is because the child thinks they are following instructions.

Young children do not have a developed sense of abstract thought. They think in visual terms. "Food" is visual, "floor" is visual, the act of throwing is visual, but the words "do not" are an abstract thought. They have no visual tie back to anything for the child to reference. Rather than using abstract words, the more effective or correct message to the child is, "Keep the food on the tray."

This applies to us adults too. Remember that most advertising messages are being read, listened to, or seen by someone passively, meaning they are not giving the message 100 percent of their attention.

What abstracts are you using in your communications? How can they be repositioned into a visual construct? While this is not always possible, it should be pursued whenever possible.

X

PULLING IT ALL TOGETHER

We have covered many concepts and ideas within these pages, but the real proof comes with making it work, essentially proving that these are more than just theories but that they have practical use.

This section of the book will focus on showing these concepts, dissecting them, and explaining how these principles have already worked in a real-life advertising situation. These are real examples that have generated millions of dollars in business.

EXAMPLES

BACKAID MAX

As the name indicates, this product's purpose is to address back pain. The challenge here was to create a low-cost advertising campaign that would drive sales for a product that competes in a very crowded space: pain relief. Our first step was to understand the buyer and to understand the formula, specifically what claims the product could make and what would be the most important features to call out to this demographic.

With a relatively modest budget, we chose to promote this client on Sirius/XM satellite radio. Here is the script:

> If you've got lower back pain, that sharp ache makes it hard to drive—stabbing pain through your back with every bump in the road. And that awful, pinching pain can radiate down, shooting pins and needles into your legs.

> Finally, there's good news. A truly unique and effective formula called BACKAID Max is available now at CVS and Walgreens.

> BACKAID Max is aspirin-free with two powerful medicines that effectively relieve temporary minor lower back and leg pain.

Plus, it helps relieve the pressure-related pain that can make discomfort radiate into your legs—like with sciatica.

BACKAID's six-hour formula provides maximum strength, over-the-counter pain relief.

That's why customers consistently rate BACKAID five stars for how well it reduces their back pain and pressure.

You've been waiting long enough for effective relief from lower back and leg pain. Join the many people who have found the five-star relief they need with specially formulated BACKAID Max.

Pull into a CVS or Walgreens now to get BACKAID Max in the blue box in the pain relief aisle.

**Use as directed.

Now let us look at this script again and break it down line-by-line.

If you've got lower back pain,

This speaks directly to the listener as if it is a one-on-one conversation. This allows the listener to self-identify if the message applies to them, narrowing down the audience, and identifies it as a very important message for those with lower back pain.

> that sharp ache makes it hard to drive—stabbing pain through your back with every bump in the road. And that awful, pinching pain can radiate down, shooting pins and needles into your legs.

This line incorporates visualization or theater of the mind. It allows us to leverage unpleasant memories that the listener may have had in the past. Also, by using language in the present tense, we are presupposing or deciding on the listener's past.

> Finally, there's good news. A truly unique and effective formula called BACKAID Max is available now at CVS and Walgreens.

We start off disrupting the listener with the good news, leveraging a PGO spike. Within that moment we deliver the brand name followed by the "available now at CVS" line. This comment gives the listener the feeling that it was not available previously, indicating it is new or a very hot seller.

> BACKAID Max is aspirin-free with two powerful medicines that effectively relieve temporary minor lower back and leg pain.

In this line you see the technique of multiplication through subtraction. Since aspirin causes problems for some people, we are focusing on what it does not have, and referencing what it does have as "two powerful" ingredients.

Then we narrow the focus down to a very personal level of back and leg pain, so the listener can decide that this is just for them and their need. (Note that these ingredients would also work for other pain, but the specificity of our indication makes it more desirable.)

The word "temporary" is slid in very quickly for the purpose of meeting FDA language requirements.

> Plus, it helps relieve the pressure-related pain that can make discomfort radiate into your legs—like with sciatica.

The purpose of this line is to create more mental theater and to get the listener to re-experience these pains. This also leans into people's natural tendency to find themselves in nearly any set of symptoms. You will also notice we say "like sciatica." The reason is because these drugs do not have an approval for the treatment of sciatica (even though it does work well), so we reference it with the modifier "like."

> BACKAID's six-hour formula provides maximum strength, over-the-counter pain relief. That's why customers consis-

tently rate BACKAID five stars for how well it reduces their back pain and pressure.

This is the major anchor point in this radio spot. We start by demonstrating that it lasts for six hours, which indicates strong relief. Knowing that people seek results, we promote maximum strength. To reassure it is the best, we focus in on "over-the-counter," giving the consumer the idea that it may have been prescription in the past, but they now can get it without a doctor visit. Finally, we add the social proof; explaining that the product gets five-star reviews, which leans into the herd mentality that the world is smarter than I am and knows what works.

> You've been waiting long enough for effective relief from lower back and leg pain. Join the many people who have found the five-star relief they need with specially formulated BACKAID Max.

This line starts with a presupposition and is resetting the listener's past by telling them they have been "waiting long enough." This line also leverages people's belief that they are deserving of good things. We again remind them of the specificity of the indication and press right back into social proof by telling them to "join" the others who got "five-star relief." This line also assumes the listeners' future.

Pull into a CVS or Walgreens now to get BACKAID Max in the blue box in the pain relief aisle.

This last line in the radio spot is an embedded command instructing the unconscious mind what they are to do: "Pull into a CVS or Walgreens now." That command is hidden by immediately telling the listener what color the box is and where to find the product in the store. This also makes sure that there will be no confusion when they arrive at the store shelf.

**Use as directed.

The final legal requirement is added in a different tone and speed to disconnect it from the rest of the spot. People are used to hearing and dismissing these required legal messages and they do not typically interfere with the rest of the ad messaging.

The results of this spot were nearly a 25 percent jump in sales, and the client more than doubled their spend for the next advertising cycle.

NAUZENE

This is a campaign for a client who makes a competing product to Pepto Bismol, which is a category giant. Our client did not have the resources to advertise 52 weeks a year, so we built a campaign around indulgent holidays, such as New Year's Eve, Super Bowl, St. Patrick's Day, Memorial Day, Fourth of July, Labor Day, Halloween, Thanksgiving, and Christmas. There are two talents. Here is the script:

(Announcer): It's time to play: Vomit or No Vomit? Brought to you by Nauzene.

(Announcer): Question for Andy: It was the party of the year, made better by frozen pizza at 4:00 a.m. until your stomach turned into a churning mess of New Year's regret.

(Announcer): Do you A: Vomit? B: Drink the pink stuff? C: Take fast-acting Nauzene?

(Andy): TAKE Nauzene!

(Announcer): Correct! Nauzene's four-minute formula quickly relieves stomach discomfort from overindulging.

Get Nauzene NOW in the purple box at Walmart or your favorite store.

Now let us look at this script again and break it down line-by-line.

(Announcer): It's time to play: Vomit or No Vomit? Brought to you by Nauzene.

There is a lot going on in this short sentence. The spot is recorded to sound like the opening to a game show with music and a big announcer voice. This gives the spot a feel of familiarity, which leverages framing effect, but then the name is *Vomit or No Vomit?* which causes an immediate PGO spike, forcing the listener into a transderivational search for a former memory that will make sense of this.

While this valuable moment of the conscious mind being offline occurs, we drive the brand name into the memory. Finally, the use of the word "vomit" causes the listener to trigger visual memory, recalling their own experience of vomiting.

An example would be if I said, "Don't think of a pink elephant." Your memory will be triggered to recall and will create a visual of a pink elephant, even if only to attempt to not think about it.

> (Announcer): Question for Andy: It was the party of the year, made better by frozen pizza at 4:00 a.m. until your stomach turned into a churning mess of New Year's regret.

What is at play here is the description of an event that the listener is probably going to participate in—an NYE party. We then create the stomach-churning story to remind them of the past.

Do you A: Vomit?

This is recorded with a soundtrack of people making disgusted sighing sounds, reinforcing the listeners' own memory of the last time they vomited.

B: Drink the pink stuff?

When you hear these words, the audience's sounds of disgust get louder, as if using the pink stuff was somehow worse than vomiting. Most people have taken the pink stuff while sick, which already relates it to a bad event. But by reinforcing this through sound effects, we are neuro-associating our client's competitor with vomiting, making the competition not only inferior, but off-putting.

C: Take fast-acting Nauzene?

These words are accompanied by soothing, gleeful audience approval. The unconscious message is that people like taking this product. This is the implied social proof.

(Andy): *TAKE Nauzene!*

(Announcer): Correct! Nauzene's four-minute formula quickly relieves stomach discomfort from overindulging.

Here the audience is reassured that C is the right answer,

which they have already answered in the mind. It also calls out the four-minute results, which play into hyperbolic thinking, and neuro-associates our product with successfully feeling better.

Get Nauzene NOW in the purple box at Walmart or your favorite store.

This last line in the spot is a direct command, in addition to being a call to action. Like the previous example, the listener is told the color of the box to aid in finding it on the store shelf.

This campaign is in its third year of running with some modifications and continues to break sales records every holiday.

DERMEND

Our next example is an advertorial for the brand DerMend. This is a line of products with the unifying message that the brand provides skin care products for mature adults. We chose to use newspaper print with the *Parade* magazines since demographically we know this is the 65-plus demo.

The advertorial model is a great tool when you have a product or service that needs some time to explain regardless of it being in print or online. This content model allows the advertiser to spend more time with the consumer.

The key to good content or advertorials is that every sentence needs to draw the reader into the following sentence.

As we look at the headline, "Finally, a Company Dedicated to Senior Skincare Needs," we see seven words or less, not counting articles of speech. The reason for this is that if there are more than seven words, most people start reading from left to right, whereas with seven words or less they can consume the headline as a phrase. Also, remember that our conscious mind can handle only seven bits of information, plus or minus two.

The next thing we focus on in this headline is having the hook that will attract the reader to engage with the story. In this case we use a universal truth. We know from experience and surveys that most seniors feel that skin care companies are focused on the young or even the middle-aged, ignoring the needs of seniors. This universal truth headline creates an "Aha!" moment for the reader: first, that someone acknowledges what they have always suspected and second, excitement that someone finally cares.

In the first line of copy, what do you see? Another universal truth. "As we age our skin experiences dramatic change and needs special care." Most seniors will agree that their body has changed and has different needs.

We then repeat the idea, but directly this time, "but the big skincare companies aren't paying attention to us." This is a line that gets people a bit angry, that addresses how they have been ignored, and it leads to getting a mental agreement from the reader.

Next comes a line about how easily they can get bruised, a highly relatable event that causes the reader to mentally create their own version of bruising and how easily it happens.

What you should notice here is that we immediately drove three universal truths in a row. This is referred to in hypnosis as a "yes set." It is based on Newton's second law: "A thing in motion tends to stay in motion until acted upon by an outside force." In hypnosis this is used to induce hypnosis more quickly. The hypnotherapist would ask three or four questions in a row that would require an obvious yes answer, thus creating a pattern or behavior of saying yes. An example would be, "Are you here today to quit smoking?" "Do you want to stop smoking today?" and "If we can delete your desire for cigarettes, would that be a good outcome for you?"

Notice that it would be silly for the person to say anything but yes (assuming they came in for smoking cessation). But the continuing drive to get them to say yes keeps them in a mood or state likely to continue saying yes.

The same thing is happening in this advertorial. The reader is following through a list of comments to which they are likely to say yes. Not only does it build rapport with the reader by demonstrating that we understand them, but it also puts them into a yes set or compliance mode.

Next in the copy we use theater of the mind, recreating conditions they have likely experienced and presupposing or reframing their past experiences such as "see wrinkly, loose, sagging skin." Once we have gained their attention, created a yes or compliance set, built rapport, and defined their specific problems, we now demonstrate how the brand is the solution to their now well-defined problem. "Fortunately, one company has pledged to help mature adults deal with common skin problems." We are literally offering them hope and relief for a problem that was not even on their mind one minute ago.

As you read further through the document, you will see the heavy use of salience with phrases and words such as "one-of-a-kind" and "recommended by dermatologists." After completing the product descriptions, we move to embedded commands telling them to "learn more" at the website and to "find the products at" retailers.

The results of this ad have been astounding, often resulting in some stores running out of product.

WAX-RX

Wax-Rx is an ear wax removal kit that sells for 400 percent of the price of its closest competitor. It is $40 compared to $8.99. We chose to use a television commercial because first, this is a highly demonstrable product and second, television is an in-home media. This is an in-home use product and the closer we can reach a consumer at the point of consumption, the better.

The goal of the commercial was to demonstrate to consumers that although this was four times the price of other offerings, it was worth it because it works, and the other products do not.

A man struggles to clean his ear with a cotton swab, showing obvious discomfort.

Voiceover:

"Do you feel like the way you clean your ears at home doesn't work well enough?

This spot immediately starts off with the "Feel, Felt, Found" model of neuro-linguistic programming. "Do you feel like the way you clean your ears at home doesn't work well enough?"

This line immediately acknowledges for the viewer that their feelings matter. Next, the vague language of "well enough" allows the consumer to be the final word on what is successful and what is not.

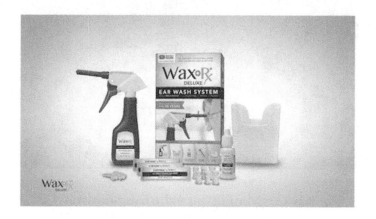

Cut to Product shot / graphic of Wax-Rx Ear Wash System

Voiceover:

"I felt the same way. But then I tried the Wax-Rx ear wash system.

The next line is the felt model. "I felt the same way." The consumer has now found an ally, someone who agrees with them and lets them know it is not just them and that they are perfectly normal.

The next line is the found statement. "But then I tried the Wax-Rx ear wash system."

Cut back to Man using / showing how to properly use the Wax-Rx Ear Wash System.

Voiceover:

"Wax-Rx was designed by a doctor and is the same system used in medical clinics."

The next line, "Wax-Rx was designed by a doctor and is the same system used in medical clinics," provides expertise or prestige. Then the script immediately jumps into social proof that this is commonly used by medical clinics.

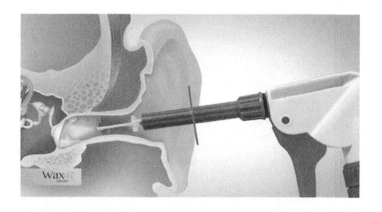

Graphic of inner ear, and how Wax-Rx
works to remove harmful ear wax.

Voiceover:

*"The re-useable Wax-Rx system has
everything you need to effectively remove
ear wax at home without the inconvenience
of a doctor's visit.*

"The reusable Wax-Rx system has everything you need
to effectively remove ear wax at home without the inconvenience of a doctor visit." We lead off here with a value
proposition of "reusable" and "everything you need." Then
we immediately follow it up with a solution to a fear many
people have, which is going to a doctor.

Final product shot

Voiceover:

*"You should use the Doctor trusted Wax-Rx
ear wash system you can get it now at
Walgreens or Wax-Rx.com.*

"You should use the doctor-trusted Wax-Rx system." The
last line contains two embedded commands, "You should
use" and "get it now." These are then surrounded by softer
language to give them cover.

The results of this ad are that the sales have already
exceeded Walgreens' expectations by 500 percent.

XI

CONCLUSION

As you now know, people frequently do not make buying decisions for logical reasons. In many cases, individuals do not even realize or understand why they purchase the things that they do. This is why *Hypno-tising,* the combination of hypnosis and advertising, came to be.

The content of this book was to demonstrate that by using neuro-linguistic programming, behavioral science, and hypnotic patterns, advertisers and marketers can leverage people's nonlogical buying triggers or reasons to improve the results of advertising and commercial communications.

Great communications should be crafted in a fashion that will help or assist consumers in overcoming their own built-in biases and fears and to lean into the mental short-cuts or heuristics of the consumer and motivate them to explore life-improving products and services. By understanding this we can create communications that reach our consumer at a much deeper and unconscious level.

While some people challenge the ethics of using such subliminal techniques to influence people, evidence shows that regardless of the underlying techniques employed in communications, it is nearly impossible to sell something to someone who has no need for it.

So, what will you do with your newfound knowledge? The thing about learning is, once we acquire new knowledge, we can never go back to where we once were. By now you should be looking at advertising messages completely differently, either trying to discover the underlying psychology of the ad or realizing that most advertising is poorly crafted.

As you now spend time talking to so-called "advertising experts," you may start to realize that way too many people in our industry have come to the discipline as frustrated writers or movie makers, unable to make a living in the entertainment world.

Advertising that is not specifically created to move consumers to action and to sell more products or services is nothing more than company-sponsored entertainment. Think of the times when you have seen a really creative or funny ad and want to share it with friends, but for the life of you, you cannot remember the company being advertised. That's not advertising, that's entertainment.

Although creating great ads does require a high level of artistic ability, it is useless if the underpinnings of the communication are not based on solid neuroscience. Our goal for this book is no different than a great ad—it is to make you think differently and to change you. This goal is achieved if you refuse to waste any more advertising dollars on paid entertainment, and if you use this knowledge to help you hold advertising agencies and consultants to the highest standard—which is not them winning awards for clever ads, it is to help you sell more stuff, to more people, more often, for more money.

ACKNOWLEDGMENTS

Writing a book isn't easy and is rarely the effort of just one person. It really takes a community of support to make it happen. This book would not be possible without my wife, Sally. She is the person who had the vision to push me out of my comfort zone and who also identified what my true unique ability is. Without her, I would be a really smart dreamer with nothing to show for it.

To Michelle Pike, who for decades has played the role of consigliere, confidant, sounding board, and editor. Without your help and input this book would look like an explosion in a steel wool factory. I also want to thank members of the Jekyll and Hyde team, Jenn Hill for her great illustrations and Daniel Banas for thoughtful creative input.

And to my daughter Andi, because...well...you're Andi.

Finally, it goes without saying that any work like this is built by standing on the shoulders of giants. Some of these people have made contributions that have changed the way we see the world, while others are people close to me that have directly influenced my thinking. To these people, I offer a special thank you for motivating and supporting me, including Dr. Mike Mandel, Dan Sullivan, Chuck Woolery, Mel Partovich Esq, Dr. Jeffrey Gladden, and many, many great and wonderful friends that I am so blessed to have.

ABOUT THE AUTHOR

DR. MARK YOUNG is one of those rare individuals with an insatiable thirst for knowledge. He reserves at least two hours per day to study, staying on top of trends in technology, human behavior, geopolitics, physics, economics, and future studies. His unusual style of processing information and problem solving was formed early on, based on his own combination of epistemology and multidisciplinary thinking.

Mark is a serial entrepreneur with current interests in advertising, real estate development, and media. He leveraged his education and passion of neuroscience, persuasion, NLP, and hypnosis to build Jekyll+Hyde Labs into one of the nation's most successful advertising agencies for challenger and emerging brand consumer products.

He is the co-host of both one of the nation's top news and politics podcasts and a show on life extension where he teaches people his plan to live beyond 120 years of age. He also believes in making the world a better place and serves on the board of World Mission, which provides humanitarian aid, education, and faith-based training across the planet.

TAKING A DIFFERENT PATH

When other kids looked up to superheroes or performers, Mark was studying everything he could about Ben Franklin, Thomas Edison, and Blaise Pascal. Mark has lived by the words of these men, especially Pascal, who said, "As we cannot be universal by knowing everything there is to know about everything, we must know a little about everything, because it is much better to know something about everything than everything about something."

The word that best describes Mark's personality is "passion." As laser focused as Mark is on the success of his businesses, he is equally obsessed with new experiences and learning. He is currently working toward his professional race car driver's license, and enjoys flying planes, as well as road trips on his motorcycle. He plans to one day soar the skies in a jet-propelled wingsuit.

The genesis of *Hypno-tising* is from Young's doctoral thesis,

Leveraging Neuro-Linguistic Programming, Hypnotic Patterns and Behavioral Science to Trigger Consumer Response.

Mark resides in Michigan and Florida with his wife, Sally.

He can be contacted at myoung@JandHLabs.com.

REFERENCES

Albarracin, D. & Mitchell, A.L. (2004). The role of defensive confidence in preference for pro-attitudinal information: How believing that one is strong can sometimes be a defensive weakness. *Personality and Social Psychology Bulletin*, 30(12), 1565-1584.

Anxiety and depression (1979). Anxiety and Depression Association of America. Retrieved June 10, 2020 from https://adaa.org/.

Averbeck, J., Jones, A. & Robertson, P. (2011, February 2). Knowledge and health messages: An examination of affect as heuristics and information as systematic processing for fear appeals. *Southern Communication Journal*, 76, 35-54.

Baron, J. (2008). *Thinking and deciding.* (4th ed.). New York: Cambridge University Press, 47-48.

Baron, R., Vandello, J. & Brunsman, B. (1996, January 1). The forgotten variable in conformity research: Impact of task importance on social influence. *Journal of Personality and Social Psychology*, 71(5), 915-927.

Beer, J. (2019, September 19). One year later what did we learn from Nike's blockbuster Colin Kaepernick ad? *Fast Company*. Retrieved June 10, 2020, from https://www.fastcompany.com/90399316/one-year-later-what-did-we-learn-from-nikes-blockbuster-colin-kaepernick-ad.

Bernoulli, D. (1954). Exposition of a New Theory on the Measurement of Risk. *Econometrica*. 22(1), 23–36.

Bolkan, S, & Andersen, P. (2009). Image introduction and social influence: Explanation and initial tests. *Journal of Basic and Applied Social Psychology*, Vol 32(4), 317–324.

Bonnet, L., Comte, A., Tatu, L., Millot, J., Moulin, T. & Medeiros, E. (2015, July 5). The role of the amygdala in the perception of positive emotions: an "intensity detector." *Frontiers in Behavioral Neuroscience*, 9(178).

Boyer, D.M. (2018, January). Scaling of bony canals for encephalic vessels in euarchontans: Implications for the role of the vertebral artery and brain metabolism. *Journal of Human Evolution*, 114, 85–101.

BT06 Dialog 02—Metaphor—Kottler & Lankton. (2006, December 8). The Milton H. Erickson Foundation. Retrieved June 30, 2020 from https://catalog.erickson-foundation.org/item/bt06-dialog-02-metaphor-kottler-lankton-49233.

BT10 Fundamentals of Hypnosis 04—The Principle of Utilization in Ericksonian Hypnotherapy. (2010, December 10). The Milton H. Erickson Foundation. Retrieved June 30, 2020 from https://catalog.erickson-foundation.org/item/bt10-fundamentals-hypnosis-04-principle-utilization-ericksonian-hypnotherapy-20731.

Chernev, B. & Goodman, J. (2015, April). Choice overload: A conceptual review and meta-analysis. *Journal of Consumer Psychology*, 25(2), 333–358.

Chomsky, N. (1957). *Syntactic Structures*. Mountan & Co.—*Cognitive Bias*. (2005, June). Wikipedia. Retrieved June 3, 2020, from https://en.wikipedia.org/wiki/Cognitive_bias.

Cialdini, R. (1984). *Influence: The Psychology of Persuasion*. William Morrow and Company, Inc., 114–165.

Cialdini, R. (2016). *Pre-Suasion: A revolutionary way to influence and persuade*. Simon & Shuster, 105–122.

Cialdini, R., Borden, R., Thorne, A., Walker, M., Freeman, S., & Sloan, Lloyd R. (1974). Basking in the reflected glory: Three football field studies. *Journal of Personality and Social Psychology*, 34, 366–375.

De Dreu, C. (2012) Oxytocin modulates cooperation within competition between groups: An integrative review and research agenda. *Hormones and Behavior*, 61(3), 419–428.

Dunning, D. & Kruger, J. (1999). Unskilled and unaware of it: How difficulties in recognizing one's own incompetence leads to inflated self-assessments. *Journal of Personality and Social psychology*, 77(6), 1121–1134.

Efferson, C., Lalive, R., & Fehr, E. (2008, September 26). The Coevolution of cultural groups and ingroup favoritism. *Science*, 321(5897), 1844–1849.

Finucane, M.L., Alhakami, A., Slovic, P. & Johnson, S.M. (2000). The affect heuristic in judgment of risks and benefits. *Journal of Behavioral Decision Making* 13(1), 1–17.

Freud, S. (1895). The project for a scientific psychology.

Harshaw, R. (2014). Marketing solutions for remodelers: Monopolize your marketplace. Retrieved March 31, 2020, from https://mymonline.com.

Hawthorne Effect—Definition, History, and Latest Research. Corporate Finance Institute. Retrieved June 29, 2020, from https:// corporatefinanceinstitute.com/resources/careers/ soft-skills/ hawthorne-effect.

Holt, J. (2011, November 27). Two brains running, *The New York Times,* 16.

Iyengar, L. & Lepper, M. (2000). When choice is demotivating, can one desire too much of a good thing? *Journal of Personality and Social Psychology,* 79(6), 995-1006.

Kahneman, D. (2011). *Thinking, fast and slow.* Farrar, Straus, and Giroux.

Kahneman, D. & Tversky, A. (1974, September 27). Judgment under uncertainty: Heuristics and biases. *Science,* 185 (4157), 1124-1131.

Kahneman, D. & Tversky, A. (1986) Rational choice and the framing of decisions. *Journal of Business,* 59(4), 251.

Klayman, J. & Ha, Y. (1987, April) Confirmation, disconfirmation and information in hypothesis testing. *Psychological Review* 94(2), 211-228.

Kunda, Z. (1999) *Social Cognition; Making Sense of People.* MIT Press, 101-113 & 112-115.

Langer, E. J. (1989) *Mindfulness.* Da Capo.

Lord, C., Ross, L. & Lepper, M. (1979). Biased assimilation and attitude polarization: The effects of prior theories on subsequently considered evidence. *Journal of Personality and Social Psychology,* 37(11), 2098-2099.

Mandel, M. (2020, June 11). *Architecture of hypnosis system.* Mike Mandel Hypnosis. Retrieved April 28, 2020 from https:// mikemandelhypnosis.com/.

Mandel, M. (2020, June 11). *Live and online hypnosis training and personal development.* Mike Mandel Hypnosis. Retrieved April 28, 2020 from https://mikemandelhypnosis.com/.

Media Dynamics Inc., America's Media Usage and Ad Exposure: 1945–2014.

Miller, G.A. (1956). The magical number seven, plus or minus two: Some limits on our capacity for processing information. *Psychological Review,* 63(2), 81–97.

Milton H. Erickson. Wikipedia. Retrieved June 29, 2020 from en.wikipedia.org/wiki/Milton_H._Erickson.

National Research Council (US), Committee on Future Directions for Behavioral and Social Sciences Research at the National Institute of Health; In B.H. Singer & C.D. Ryff (Eds.) (2001). *National Academies Press.*

Platow, M.J., Haslam, S.A., Both, A., Chew, I., Cuddon, M., Goharpey, N., Maurer, J., Rosini, S., Tsekouras, A., & Grace, D.M. (2005) "It's not funny if *they're* laughing": Self-categorization, social influence and responses to canned laughter. *Journal of Experimental Social Psychology.* 41(5), 550.

Richard Bandler Live Webinar (2019, September 13). *YouTube.* Retrieved June 30, 2020 from https://www.youtube.com/watch?v=Miy69HMf6cM.

Russel, D. & Jones, W. (1980). When superstition fails: Reactions to disconfirmation of paranormal beliefs. *Personality and Social Psychology Bulletin,* 6(1), 83–88.

Shafir, E. (1993). Choosing versus rejecting: Why some options are both better and worse than others. *Memory and Cognition,* 21(4), 546–556.

Simon, H. (1957). *Models of man: Social and rational mathematical essays on rational human behavior in a social setting.* (1st ed.). John Wiley and Sons, Inc.

Stanton, S., Sinnott-Armstrong, Walter, & Huettel, S. (2014, October 26). *Journal of Business Ethics*.

Straw, B. (1976, June). Knee deep in the big muddy: A study of escalating commitment to a chosen course of action. *Organizational Behavior & Human Performance*, 16(1), 27–44.

Swann, W., Pelham, B. & Krull, D. (1989). Agreeable fancy or disagreeable truth? Reconciling self-enhancement and self-verification. *Journal of Personality and Social Psychology*, 57(5), 782–791.

Tart, C. (2001). *Waking Up: Overcoming the obstacles to human potential.* iUniverse, 27–49.

The Power of Because: It's a Persuasive Word That Explains Why. (n.d.). Word Wise. Retrieved June 29, 2020 from www. nonprofitcopywriter.com/power-of-because.html.